An anchor for the soul

Hebrews

by Michael J. Kruger

Hebrews For You

These studies are adapted from *Hebrews For You*. If you are reading *Hebrews For You* alongside this Good Book Guide, here is how the studies in this booklet link to the chapters of *Hebrews For You*:

Study One → Ch 1
Study Two → Ch 2-3
Study Three → Ch 3-4
Study Four → Ch 4-5

Study Five → Ch 6
Study Six → Ch 7-9
Study Seven → Ch 9-11
Study Eight → Ch 11-13

Find out more about *Hebrews For You* at:
www.thegoodbook.com/for-you

Hebrews: An Anchor for the Soul
The Good Book Guide to Hebrews
© Michael J. Kruger/The Good Book Company, 2021
Series Consultants: Tim Chester, Tim Thornborough,
          Anne Woodcock, Carl Laferton

Published by:
The Good Book Company

thegoodbook.com | thegoodbook.co.uk
thegoodbook.com.au | thegoodbook.co.nz | thegoodbook.co.in

ISBN: 9781784986049

Printed in Turkey

CONTENTS

Introduction: Good Book Guides

Every Bible-study group is different—yours may take place in a church building, in a home or in a cafe, on a train, over a leisurely mid-morning coffee or squashed into a 30-minute lunch break. Your group may include new Christians, mature Christians, non-Christians, moms and tots, students, businessmen or teens. That's why we've designed these *Good Book Guides* to be flexible for use in many different situations.

Our aim in each session is to uncover the meaning of a passage, and see how it fits into the "big picture" of the Bible. But that can never be the end. We also need to appropriately apply what we have discovered to our lives. Let's take a look at what is included:

⊕ **Talkabout:** Most groups need to "break the ice" at the beginning of a session, and here's the question that will do that. It's designed to get people talking around a subject that will be covered in the course of the Bible study.

⟨⟩ **Investigate:** The Bible text for each session is broken up into manageable chunks, with questions that aim to help you understand what the passage is about. The **Leader's Guide** contains **guidance for questions**, and sometimes ⊻ additional "follow-up" questions.

⟨⟩ **Explore more (optional):** These questions will help you connect what you have learned to other parts of the Bible, so you can begin to fit it all together like a jig-saw; or occasionally look at a part of the passage that's not dealt with in detail in the main study.

→ **Apply:** As you go through a Bible study, you'll keep coming across **apply** sections. These are questions to get the group discussing what the Bible teaching means in practice for you and your church. ⟨⟩ **Getting personal** is an opportunity for you to think, plan and pray about the changes that you personally may need to make as a result of what you have learned.

↑ **Pray:** We want to encourage prayer that is rooted in God's word—in line with his concerns, purposes and promises. So each session ends with an opportunity to review the truths and challenges highlighted by the Bible study, and turn them into prayers of request and thanksgiving.

The **Leader's Guide** and introduction provide historical background information, explanations of the Bible texts for each session, ideas for **optional extra** activities, and guidance on how best to help people uncover the truths of God's word.

Why study Hebrews?

As you read the book of Hebrews, you very quickly become aware that its author just loves Jesus Christ. He thinks he is amazing, magnificent, extraordinary; he thinks he is all in all.

We all experience times when we stop feeling like that—when we are following Jesus out of duty instead of delight in how wonderful he is. At those times it is easy to look over at something else—some other person, situation, or way of living—and think, "That looks better."

But the book of Hebrews shows us that *Jesus* is better.

The book, which has an unnamed author, was likely written in the early AD 60s. It is a letter to the "Hebrews"—which is just another name for the Jewish people. The audience is primarily Jewish Christians who grew up in Judaism but have believed in Jesus. They have embraced him as the Messiah but are thinking about turning back to the old ways: animal sacrifices and worship at the temple.

So our author gives them—and us—a doctrinal anchor: a clear, detailed understanding of why Jesus is better than anything else. He includes six warnings, which follow the same simple theme: don't drift away. The book is designed to keep us walking with him on the right path—the path to life.

Before embarking on this journey, you should know that the book of Hebrews is not a light appetizer. It is more like a porterhouse steak. The author talks a lot about how Jesus' sacrifice is superior to the sacrifices made in the Old Testament—requiring us to think hard about the structure and complexity of the old covenant system. It's meaty stuff. But it's wonderful stuff. The book of Hebrews ranges across the Old Testament and shows us how Christ fulfilled it all. As you will see in each of these eight studies, he is the crescendo of God's work on earth. My prayer for you is that, in a fresh and new way, as you read Hebrews you will fall in love with Christ all over again.

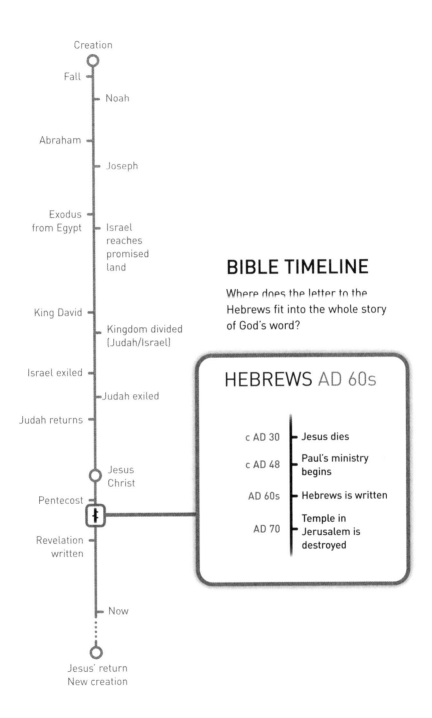

Creation

Fall

Noah

Abraham

Joseph

Exodus from Egypt

Israel reaches promised land

King David

Kingdom divided (Judah/Israel)

Israel exiled

Judah exiled

Judah returns

Jesus Christ

Pentecost

Revelation written

Now

Jesus' return New creation

BIBLE TIMELINE

Where does the letter to the Hebrews fit into the whole story of God's word?

HEBREWS AD 60s

c AD 30 — Jesus dies

c AD 48 — Paul's ministry begins

AD 60s — Hebrews is written

AD 70 — Temple in Jerusalem is destroyed

1

Hebrews 1:1-14
JESUS IN ALL HIS GLORY

⊕ talkabout

1. Do you think people in our world today expect to hear from God? If they do, how do they think he will speak?

⊕ investigate

▶ **Read Hebrews 1:1-4**

2. The first two verses tell us twice that God has spoken. What are the differences between the way God spoke in verse 1 and the way he spoke in verse 2?

3. What do verses 2-3 tell us about the Son's power?

4. What do these verses tell us about how the Son reveals God?

5. What do these verses tell us about what the Son came to do?

→ apply

6. We think of Jesus as our Savior from sin. But these verses remind us that he is also the sovereign King of everything. How will it change our lives if we remember this?

⊡ investigate

7. What is the comparison in verse 4?

It seems as though the audience of this letter has begun to honor and venerate angels so that they took the place of Jesus for them. This may seem irrelevant to us at first, but in fact it doesn't matter what the particular distraction is.

What impresses you? What do you prize above other things? Is there anything you tend to think would make your life just right?

Think back to these answers as you read the rest of Hebrews 1, and examine your heart. Is there any way in which you are too easily pleased by the things of the world? How do they compare to Christ?

⟩ **Read Hebrews 1:5-14**

8. In verses 5-6, how do we know that Jesus is better than angels?

> **DICTIONARY**
>
> **Begotten (v 5):** become the father of.
> **Scepter (v 8):** a symbol of royal power.
> **Anointed (v 9):** in ancient times, oil was smeared or poured onto a person's head (especially a king's) as a sign of honor or celebration.
> **Perish (v 11):** die.
> **Garment (v 11):** piece of clothing.
> **Ministering (v 14):** serving.

⊡ **explore more**

optional

Verses 5-6 could make it seem as though there was a time when Jesus was not the Son, and then a point when he became the Son. If God can say, "Today I have begotten you" and call Jesus his "firstborn," doesn't that imply that Jesus is secondary or inferior to the Father?

Nothing could be further from the truth. The Son shares in the same eternal, divine nature as the Father. He has always been the Son.

⟩ **Read Acts 13:32-33 and Romans 1:4**

What, for Paul, is the key event that declares Jesus to be God's Son?

9. What is the Son's role in verse 8?

10. What role do the angels have, meanwhile (v 7, 14)?

11. Re-read verses 7-14. How else do we see Jesus' superiority?

⊕ apply

12. What do we tend to value the most—and how do those things compare to Jesus? How will this comparison change the way you think about or act toward those things?

⊕ pray

Make a list of all the ways in which Jesus is described in this chapter—the roles and qualities he has and the things he has done.

Pray through your list together, worshiping Jesus for all that he is.

2 Hebrews 2:1 – 3:6
A GREAT SALVATION

The story so far

Jesus Christ is supreme over all things—he is the ultimate revelation of God. Our response should be simple: to give glory to God and to worship Christ.

⊕ talkabout

1. When in life do you have to pay attention? When are you good at doing so, and when is it more difficult? Why?

⊕ investigate

> **Read Hebrews 2:1-13**

2. The author speaks about "a great salvation" in verse 3. What reasons does he give in verses 1-4 to pay attention to this message of salvation?

DICTIONARY

Transgression (v 2): sin.
Retribution (v 2): punishment.
Attested (v 3): confirmed by a witness.
Subject (v 5): put under the control of.
Sanctify (v 11): make holy.

In verses 5-8, the author explains more about this message of salvation. He does this by quoting from Psalm 8.

3. Verse 6 talks about "man": the human race. What does the quotation in verses 6-8 tell us about humanity's place in the world?

4. In verse 8, God's plan for humanity seems to have gone wrong. Why do you think this is? In what ways are we ruled rather than being rulers?

5. However, in verse 9, we see that this quotation is not just a description of humanity but also of one particular human. Who is it, and what has he done to make this psalm describe him so well?

• What is the result of that for us (v 9, 10)?

6. What is our identity now (v 11-13)?

➔ apply

7. This passage tells us that we were designed for glory but have fallen short of it. Discuss some of the limitations and problems that we experience as humans. What hope does this passage give us about how those things can be overcome?

⬇ investigate

▶ Read Hebrews 2:14-18

8. According to verses 14-16, why did Jesus become human?

9. What do the following things mean, and what difference do they make to our lives now?

• Jesus destroyed the one who has the power of death (v 14).

• Jesus made propitiation for sins (v 17).

• Jesus suffered when tempted (v 18).

❯ Read Hebrews 3:1-6

10. What does the author tell us to do in response to all we've heard so far (v 1, 6)?

11. To encourage us to do this, what does the author tell us about...
   • our identity (v 1, 6)?

   • Jesus' identity?

Look more carefully at the house language here.

What is the comparison in verse 3?

What does that tell us about who Jesus is (v 4)?

The imagery changes in verses 5-6. How do Moses and Jesus relate to the house now?

☷ **getting personal**

As you reflect on what this passage tells you that Jesus has done for you, what one phrase do you find particularly helpful? How does it change the way you view yourself—and others?

⤷ apply

12. The author tells us to "pay much closer attention to what we have heard" (2:1), to "consider Jesus" (3:1), and to "hold fast our confidence and our boasting in our hope" (3:6). How can you put these things into practice this week?

13. How does this passage enlarge your understanding of salvation? What do you feel most excited about?

⬆ **pray**

Spend some time praising Jesus for the "great salvation" he has achieved for us. Then turn your answers to Q12 into prayer.

Pray too for those you know who have not heard this message of salvation. Pray for them by name and ask for opportunities to share it with them.

3
Hebrews 3:7 – 4:13
IF YOU HEAR HIS VOICE

The story so far

Jesus Christ is supreme over all things, the ultimate revelation of God. Our response should be to worship him. We must also pay attention to his message of salvation. Jesus became human and died for us—not only to save us from sin, but also to make us his children and bring us to glory.

⊕ talkabout

1. How do you respond when someone doesn't really listen to you? How about when someone does listen but doesn't take what you say seriously?

⊕ investigate

> ❱ Read Hebrews 3:7-19

2. Our passage begins with a quotation (from Psalm 95:7-11). Which phrase is the key warning here?

DICTIONARY

Provoked (v 10): become angry.
Go astray (v 10): go the wrong way.
Wrath (v 11): anger.
Exhort (v 13): urge and encourage.

3. The warning involves a comparison with the generation of Israelites whom God brought out of Egypt. What did these people do (Hebrews 3:9, 16-18)?

• What was the root cause of this (v 19)?

⊡ **explore more**

optional

We find the story our author is referring to in the book of Numbers. At this point in the story, God's people are on the edge of the promised land and have sent spies to explore it.

▶ **Read Numbers 13:25 – 14:11**

Why don't the people want to enter the land?

What do Joshua and Caleb say the people are doing?

What does God say about it?

4. How did God respond (v 11, 19)?

5. How does the author apply this story to his readers (v 12-15)?

⊟ **apply**

6. What does the author tell us to do in order to avoid falling into unbelief and sin?

• How can you put this into practice?

⊡ **getting personal**

Who could you help to look to Jesus and not "be hardened by the deceitfulness of sin" (v 13) today? How will you do so?

⬇ **investigate**

▶ **Read Hebrews 4:1-13**

In the Old Testament, God's "rest" simply meant the promised land of Canaan. But in 4:1 the author makes a remarkable statement: "The promise of entering his rest still stands." Such an offer reminds us of something very critical: the ultimate rest God had in mind was never a physical plot of land.

DICTIONARY

Foundation (v 3): beginning.
David (v 7): a king and writer of psalms who lived long after the wilderness generation.
Joshua (v 8): the man who led the Israelites into the promised land.
Marrow (v 12): the inner part of a bone.

7. God's people did eventually make it to the promised land, led by Joshua. But how do verses 7-8 show that this did not fulfil God's ultimate promise of rest?

8. What is God's true rest like (v 3-4, 9-10)?

9. How do we enter it (v 1-3, 11)?

The author has been warning us to listen to God, lest we fall away like the Israelites. We, too, have the opportunity to hear God's word and believe it. Verses 12-13 tell us more about why we should listen to this word.

10. What do you think it means that God's word is...
  • "living"?

  • "active"?

  • "sharper than any two-edged sword"?

11. Do you think this is supposed to be scary or encouraging?

When are you tempted to harden your heart against God's word? Why? How does this passage help you?

⊡ apply

12.   "Today, if you hear his voice, do not harden your hearts." What implications does this have for the way we approach the Bible?

⊡ pray

Encourage one another by spending some time sharing Bible verses or passages that have been especially significant to you. Then praise God for the way he speaks through his word.

Praise God for the promise of rest for those who believe in him. Pray for anyone you know who is particularly burdened and longing for rest. Pray for anyone who especially needs help in persevering in faith while they wait for the ultimate rest of heaven.

4 HOLDING FAST

The story so far

Jesus Christ is supreme over all things, the ultimate revelation of God. Our response should be to worship him. We must also pay attention to his message of salvation. Jesus became human and died for us—not only to save us from sin, but also to make us his children and bring us to glory.

Looking back at the Israelites in the wilderness, we see the importance of hearing and obeying God's word. When we do so, we gain an eternal "rest" with God.

⊕ talkabout

1. If someone said to you, "I feel totally confident before God," how would you respond?

⊥ investigate

▶ Read Hebrews 4:14 – 5:10

2. What did a priest in Old Testament Israel do, and why was it important that they were human (5:1-2)?

DICTIONARY

Confession (4:14): what we believe.
Wayward (5:2): sinful.
Beset (v 2): troubled.
Obligated (v 3): required.
Aaron (v 4): the first high priest of Israel.
Exalt (v 5): raise up.
Melchizedek (v 6): a king and priest in ancient times.
Supplications (v 7): requests.
Reverence (v 7): respectfulness.

3. How is Jesus similar (4:15)? What events in Jesus' life do you think the author could be referring to?

- In 5:7, how does the author illustrate this? How do you think he wants you to feel when you read this verse?

4. What is the key difference between Jesus and the priests in Old Testament Israel (4:15; 5:3; 5:8-9)?

- What does this mean for us?

5. How should we respond (4:14-16)?

⊟ apply

6. How does this passage help us…

• in times of particular suffering and weakness?

• when we are tempted by sin?

• when we long for a sympathetic friend?

⊡ getting personal

What does it mean to you personally to know that Jesus can sympathize with your weaknesses?

⊡ investigate

Starting in chapter 7, the author will give us much more detail about Jesus' priesthood. He is already beginning to talk about Jesus as a high priest "after the order of Melchizedek" (5:6, 10).

But in verse 11 he interrupts himself. Before explaining his reference to Melchizedek (which we'll hear about in the next study), he pauses to address his readers directly.

▶ Read Hebrews 5:11 – 6:12

7. In 5:11-14, the author says his readers are like spiritual toddlers! What does it mean that they are living on "milk"?

DICTIONARY

Oracles (5:12): messages from God.
Discernment (v 14): ability to make good decisions.
Distinguish (v 14): tell the difference between.
Elementary (6:1): basic, foundational.
Dead works (v 1): deeds that cannot save you.
Contempt (v 6): mockery.
Cultivated (v 7): farmed.
Sluggish (v 12): slow, unenergetic.

• Why is it so important to grow in maturity and go onto "solid food" instead?

Every Christian knows the "elementary doctrine" the author describes in 6:1-2. First, "repentance" and "faith"—that's how you become a Christian. Second, "washings" and "the laying on of hands"—this is probably a reference to baptism and entrance to the church. Third, "the resurrection of the dead" and "eternal judgment" means the understanding that Christ will come again to judge the world, and that those who love him will spend eternity with him.

These are great truths. But there is so much more to learn!

However, the author now turns to a more serious warning.

8. If we believe in Jesus but then fall away, what is the result (6:4-6)?

⊡ explore more

We know from elsewhere in Scripture that it is impossible to lose your salvation once you have it (John 10:28; Ephesians 1:13-14). So, Hebrews 6:4-6 must describe someone who once seemed to be a Christian but never really was.

▶ Read Matthew 7:21-22

In this passage, how could you appear to be a true follower of Christ without really being one?

What are the similarities between the person described in Matthew 7:21-22 and the person described in Hebrews 6:4-6?

How can we make sure we are not this kind of person?

9. In the analogy in Hebrews 6:7-9, what is the equivalent of receiving but then rejecting Jesus?

- What is the author warning us that we should and should not do?

10. What "good crops" does the author describe in verses 9-12?

What "good crops" do you see in your life right now? Are you moving closer to God or further from him? In what ways do you know you need to grow?

11. What advice does he give for how to press ahead?

⊖ **apply**

12. Practically speaking, how can we find a balance between being confident in our standing before God (4:16) and yet continuing to strive for growth (6:1, 12)?

⬆ **pray**

First, thank God for the many blessings outlined in this chapter.

Then pray for one another and anyone else who is on your mind:

• Pray about how you might grow in faith and in the knowledge of him.

• Pray about how you could bear fruit by serving others.

• Ask him to help you to hold fast to Christ in every situation.

5

Hebrews 6:13 – 7:28

A SURE AND STEADFAST ANCHOR

The story so far

Jesus Christ is supreme over all things, the ultimate revelation of God. He became human and died for us to save us and bring us to glory.

Looking back at the Israelites in the wilderness, we see the importance of hearing and obeying God's word. When we do so, we gain an eternal "rest" with God.

Because of Jesus, we can draw near to God with confidence. We must persevere in faith and strive for spiritual growth.

⊕ talkabout

1. What things make it difficult to trust God and his promises?

• What "anchors" keep your faith strong in times of doubt?

⊕ investigate

The author now focuses on two figures from Old Testament history. The first is Abraham, the founding father of God's people. God made a series of promises to Abraham. For this study, the most important is the promise of a son (and ultimately many descendants). Although Abraham and his wife Sarah were too old to have children, God fulfilled his promise (Genesis 21:1-7). Their descendants became the Israelites.

▶ Read Hebrews 6:13 – 7:10

2. God promised to give Abraham many descendants. Why did Abraham know he could trust this promise (6:13-18)?

3. How is this promise relevant to us?

⊡ explore more

optional

Romans 4 explains the link between Abraham and us more fully.

▶ Read Romans 4:11-12, 16-18

God fulfilled his promise not only with physical descendants but with spiritual ones. Who is Abraham the "father" of?

4. What is the other reason to trust God here (Hebrews 6:19-20)?

Jesus is "a high priest forever after the order of Melchizedek" (v 20). But who is Melchizedek? And what does he have to do with our confidence in Christ?

Melchizedek appears in Genesis 14:17-24, when he greets Abraham after a battle. Melchizedek gives Abraham a blessing. Then Abraham gives Melchizedek a tenth (or tithe) of everything he has won in the battle.

This matters because Melchizedek is a priest, and Jesus' priesthood is "after the order of Melchizedek."

Most Old Testament priests were descendants of Abraham (specifically, descendants of Aaron, who was in the tribe of Levi, one of Abraham's great-grandsons). But Melchizedek was a priest of a different kind.

In Hebrews 7, our author argues that Melchizedek's priestly order is greater than that of Aaron. And if Melchizedek is superior to all other priests, then Christ is too.

5. How is Melchizedek described (7:1-3)? In what ways is he similar to Jesus?

6. Abraham tithed (gave a tenth of what he had won in a battle) to Melchizedek. How does this prove the superiority of Melchizedek's priesthood (v 4-6, 9-10)?

• What other proofs are given for Melchizedek's superiority (v 6-8)?

➔ apply

7. When you are doubting or uncertain, how does it help to remember that Jesus is a priest similar to Melchizedek?

⊡ getting personal

Are there any ways in which you are desperate for "refuge" (6:18) in your life at the moment? How can you keep grasping the anchor which God provides in Jesus?

⊥ investigate

▶ **Read Hebrews 7:11-28**

8. Why was a different priesthood needed (v 11, 18-19)?

DICTIONARY

Attainable (v 11): achievable.
The law (v 11): the commandments given to God's people through Moses.
Served at the altar (v 13): acted as a priest.
To the uttermost (v 25): completely or to the end.
Make intercession (v 25): speak on behalf of someone.

9. How do we know that Jesus is in "the order of Melchizedek" (v 13-17)?

10. How do we know that we can rely on this priesthood (v 20-22)?

11. What are the key differences between Jesus and the Levitical priests, and why are these differences so important for us (v 23-28)?

⊡ **getting personal**

Which areas of your life feel particularly far from being perfect? What hope does this passage give you?

⊖ **apply**

12. What are the implications of this passage for someone who is…

• frustrated by their own sin?

• doubtful or anxious?

• feeling far away from God?

⬆ pray

Lift up to God anyone you know who fits into the categories in Q12.

Then spend time praising God for promising Jesus and for keeping that promise.

6 Hebrews 8:1 – 10:25
A BETTER COVENANT

The story so far

Jesus Christ is supreme over all things, the ultimate revelation of God. He became human and died for us to save us and bring us to glory.

We must hear and obey God's word. Because of Jesus, we gain an eternal "rest" with God and can draw near with confidence. So we must persevere in faith.

Jesus is an anchor for our souls because as a priest "after the order of Melchizedek," he represents us eternally before God, giving us total security.

⊕ talkabout

1. List some different types of agreement or contract people make with one another. What happens when they are broken?

⊥ investigate

> **Read Hebrews 8:1-13**

Jesus is not just a better priest. He brings in a better covenant—a new way of relating to God. Our author now begins to compare the old covenant (the law and the sacrificial system set up by Moses) with the new covenant brought by Christ.

The old covenant was not wrong or bad. But it was a shadow of a true reality. It always looked forward to Christ.

> **DICTIONARY**
>
> **Minister (v 2):** a priest or servant.
> **Covenant (v 6):** binding agreement.
> **Mediates (v 6):** arranges an agreement between two parties.
> **Fathers (v 9):** ancestors.
> **Iniquities (v 12):** sins.
> **Obsolete (v 13):** out of date.

2. Old covenant priests made offerings in the temple (which was originally a tent). What's the difference when it comes to Jesus' ministry (v 1-6)?

In verses 8-13, the author quotes from Jeremiah 31:31-34. Hundreds of years before Jesus came, God promised a new covenant.

3. What had happened to the old covenant?

• What would this new covenant involve?

Hebrews 9 explains how Jesus' new covenant fulfilled all that the old covenant pointed toward.

9:1-10 describe what happened in the earthly tent or temple. There were two sections. The second, inner section was the most special. It was where God's presence dwelt. But it was blocked off by a curtain, because people were too sinful to be in God's presence.

Once a year, the high priest could enter the inner section to offer sacrifices for the people's sins. These sacrifices would not ultimately solve the problem. People kept on sinning. But the promised new covenant would solve the problem of sin once and for all—gaining us access to God.

> **Read Hebrews 9:11-17, 23-28**

DICTIONARY

Redemption (v 12): salvation.
Defiled (v 13): unclean.
Heifer (v 13): young cow.
Blemish (v 14): spot or defect.
Rites (v 23): ceremonies.

4. What was the blood of animals used for under the old covenant (v 13)? Why is Jesus' blood more effective?

5. What did Jesus' blood achieve (v 12, 14, 15, 26)?

(⋮) **explore more**

optional

▶ **Read Hebrews 9:18-22**

Blood has always been needed for the forgiveness of sins—because God has always been holy and someone has always had to pay.

▶ **Read Genesis 2:16-17 and Romans 6:23**

What is the result of sin here?

▶ **Read Leviticus 17:11**

Why was animal blood used to atone for sin?

▶ **Read Matthew 26:28**

Here Jesus' words echo Moses' in Hebrews 9:20. What is the difference?

(➔) **apply**

6. We can now "serve the living God" and be "eagerly waiting" for Jesus' return (v 14, 28). What do those things mean for us today?

• What might prevent us from waiting eagerly?

⊡ getting personal

"There is a fountain filled with blood
Drawn from Immanuel's veins;
And sinners, plunged beneath that flood,
Lose all their guilty stains.

"E'er since by faith I saw the stream
Thy flowing wounds supply,
Redeeming love has been my theme,
And shall be till I die." (William Cowper)

To some unbelievers, the "theme" of Jesus' blood is an ugly one. They wonder why Christians celebrate blood so much. But this theme is vital. Someone's life had to be taken in our place. It shows both the seriousness of sin and the depth of God's love for sinners.

What would you say to an unbelieving friend about the need for Christ's blood? How can you make renewed efforts to make his redeeming love your "theme"—the central idea when you speak about your faith?

⊡ investigate

❯ Read Hebrews 10:1-25

7. What did the old sacrificial system achieve, and what did it not achieve (v 1-4)?

> **DICTIONARY**
>
> **Burnt offerings and sin offerings (v 6):** two different types of animal sacrifice.
> **Assurance (v 22):** confidence.
> **Day (v 25):** the day when Christ will return.

8. What was God's perspective on the sacrifices (v 5-7)?

- These words are a quotation of Psalm 40:6-8. Christ was speaking through the psalmist (Hebrews 10:5). How do these words point to what Jesus would do?

9. In verses 15-17 the author highlights two of the promises God made in the prophecy of Jeremiah. How do verses 10-14 show that Jesus has fulfilled these promises?

10. Because of Jesus' sacrifice, what are we now able to do (v 19-22)?

11. What will help us to take hold of this hope (v 23-25)?

"Consider how to stir up one another to love and good works"
(v 24). How could you do this, and for whom, in the coming days?

➔ apply

12. Look back through Hebrews 8:1 – 10:25 and pick out a verse or verses
which you might use to encourage someone who…

• struggles with feelings of guilt.

• seeks assurance of their salvation.

• longs to be sure that God loves them.

• is confused about how the Old Testament relates to the New Testament.

• is repeatedly falling into sin.

• doubts what they believe about Jesus.

⤴ pray

"Since we have confidence to enter the holy places … let us draw near with a true heart in full assurance of faith." (Hebrews 10:19-22)

Spend some time in silent prayer, remembering that before Jesus it would have been impossible for us to enter God's presence. You may find it helpful to visualize the temple and the curtain which blocked off the inner section where God dwelt. Imagine Jesus entering on our behalf and the curtain being torn down. In the quiet, confess your sins to the One who is able to purify your conscience and bring you to God.

Then pray aloud together, praising God and bringing your prayers confidently to him.

7 Hebrews 10:26 – 12:2
THE LIFE OF FAITH

The story so far

Jesus Christ is supreme over all things, the ultimate revelation of God. He became human and died for us to save us and bring us to glory.

We must hear and obey God's word. Because of Jesus, we gain an eternal "rest" with God and can draw near with confidence. So we must persevere in faith.

Jesus is our high priest, representing us eternally before God. By his sacrifice he brought a new covenant which fixes our broken relationship with God.

⊕ talkabout

1. If you asked 100 people what the word "faith" means, what answers do you think you would get? What is helpful or unhelpful about those answers?

⊙ investigate

In Hebrews 10:22, our author urged us to draw near to God "in full assurance of faith." The remainder of chapter 10 builds on that: warning us not to turn our backs on our faith (v 26-31), the author tells us to look back at how far we've come (v 32-34) and forward to our ultimate goal (v 35-39).

"We are not of those who shrink back and are destroyed, but of those who have faith and preserve their souls," he writes in verse 39.

But what does it really mean to live by faith?

☺ explore more

> ❯ **Read Hebrews 10:26-31**

These verses say that anyone who knows about the grace of God in Christ, yet stubbornly embraces sin, is actively rejecting Christ.

Why is this so serious?

> ❯ **Read Hebrews 10:32-39**

Our author is addressing the original readers directly here.

How have they shown faith in the past (v 32-34)?

What will be the result of their faith if they persevere (v 35-39)?

> ❯ **Read Hebrews 11:1-7**

DICTIONARY

Conviction (v 1): certainty.
Heir (v 7): inheritor.

2. What does faith involve (v 1)?

• Why is faith so important (v 2, 6)?

3. What did faith look like in the lives of Abel (look up Genesis 4:1-12), Enoch (Genesis 5:18-24), and Noah (Genesis 6:9 – 7:24)?

4. What was the reward for each of these figures?

⇥ apply

5. What would it look like today for us to have faith like Abel, Enoch, and Noah?

⊡ getting personal

"Without faith it is impossible to please him" (v 6). When is it tempting to try to please God by other means? How could you live by faith in those situations?

⬇ investigate

▶ **Read Hebrews 11:8-16**

6. What did Abraham do because of his faith (v 8-9)?

DICTIONARY
Exiles (v 13): people not living in their homeland.

7. What was Abraham looking forward to (v 8, 10, 13-16)?

❯ Read Hebrews 11:17-40

8. In verses 17-19 there is another example from the life of Abraham. By faith, he obeyed God's command to offer up his only son, Isaac, as a sacrifice. Why was it difficult for Abraham to have faith and obey?

• What enabled Abraham to obey (v 19)?

9. Look at some of the other figures the author mentions. How did each one show faith? What were they looking forward to?
   • Joseph (v 22; see Genesis 50:24-25)

   • Moses (v 23-28)

   • Rahab (v 31; see Joshua 2)

10. How would you summarize the experience of people of faith in verses 32-34? What about in verses 35-38?

• Why do you think our author showed both types of experience?

All the figures we have met in Hebrews 11 were "commended through their faith" (v 39). But while they were alive they did not receive everything that was promised. They were still "looking forward."

Does that mean their faith was meaningless? No. God has provided "something better" in the new covenant. It is in Christ that all the earlier promises finally come to fruition. Now these Old Testament saints can at last be "made perfect" along with all of us who believe.

❯ **Read Hebrews 12:1-2**

11. Look at verse 2. How is Jesus' example of faith similar to the figures mentioned in chapter 11?

• But why is Jesus better than any other example of faith?

⮕ apply

12. 10:36 says, "You have need of endurance, so that when you have done the will of God you may receive what is promised." According to 12:1-2, how can we make sure we persevere in obedient faith?

13. Here are some things which make it hard to persevere in faith. For each one, how might the verses in brackets help a person in that situation?

• Struggling to believe God is there at all (11:1-3).

• Falling into the trap of seeking to please God by other means than faith in Christ (11:4-6).

• Feeling insecure and uncertain about life (11:8-10).

- Struggling to believe that God really means what he says (11:11-12, 17-19).

- Not wanting to obey God's commands (11:17-19).

- Being distracted by other things (11:16, 24-26).

- Being afraid (11:27-29).

- Feeling unworthy or insignificant (11:32-34).

- Suffering (10:34; 11:35-40).

- Becoming weighed down by sin (12:1).

⬆ pray

Praise God that it is possible for us to please him by faith.

Ask God to help you to have faith: to persevere in drawing near to him and obeying him.

Ask God to help you to fix your eyes on the final reward of being with Christ forever in the new creation.

Praise God that Jesus is the One who enables us to persevere in faith.

8

A KINGDOM THAT CANNOT BE SHAKEN

The story so far

Jesus Christ is supreme over all things, the ultimate revelation of God. He died for us to save us and bring us to an eternal "rest." We can draw near to God.

Jesus is our high priest, representing us eternally before God. By his sacrifice he brought a new covenant which fixes our broken relationship with God.

Faith in Christ is the only way to please God. Faith is practical: it means looking forward to the future God has promised and persevering in obedience.

⊕ talkabout

1. What things make people grow weary or fainthearted in their Christian life?

⊥ investigate

> **Read Hebrews 12:1-29**

The original readers of this letter have been facing all sorts of challenges. The "struggle against sin" (v 4) is not the fight against personal sins but the difficulties of living a life faithful to Jesus, enduring hostility as he did (v 3).

Looking to Jesus helps Christians to endure. But our author also encourages us to think about suffering in a different way—as discipline. A better translation might be "training." A coach may make his team run as a punishment. But he may also make them run just to build their endurance. Similarly, suffering doesn't necessarily mean that God is telling us off. But all suffering can be used by God to build our faith.

2. God is like a father (v 5-11). What is the purpose of his discipline?

• Why is suffering therefore a good sign (v 7-8)?

3. God's discipline is like athletic training (v 11-13). How should we respond—and what does that response actually look like (v 14-17)?

Persevering in faith when we are under God's discipline is difficult. But, as the remainder of chapter 12 reveals, we have the very best motivation.

Verses 18-21 describe Mount Sinai, the mountain which Moses climbed to receive the Ten Commandments. It symbolizes the entire old covenant. In verses 22-24, Mount Zion symbolizes the new covenant.

4. Compare Mount Sinai with Mount Zion.
• What kind of place is each mountain (v 18, 22, 25)?

• Who is able to go to each mountain (v 20-21, 22-23)?

- God has not changed between Mount Sinai and Mount Zion. He is still "a consuming fire" (v 29). So what *has* changed?

🔅 getting personal

How could you use this picture of two mountains to explain to an unbelieving friend the glorious good news of the gospel?

🔅 explore more

optional

Read the story of Abel to find out what it means that Jesus' blood "speaks a better word than the blood of Abel."

▶ Read Genesis 4:8-11

What do you think the blood of Abel cries out to God?

Christ's blood also "speaks" to God. What "better word" do you think it says?

5. At Mount Sinai, God's voice made the earth shake. Now he has promised to shake things again (v 26). What does this mean (v 27)?

- What will remain (v 28)?

⊡ apply

6. How should we respond to the knowledge that Jesus will one day shake the heavens and the earth (v 25, 28)?

- How does this help us to persevere in faith and pursue holiness even when times are hard or when we are tempted by other things?

7. How do you—as a church, and as individuals—usually approach God in prayer and worship? How can you make sure you do so with gratitude, reverence, and awe (v 28)?

⊡ investigate

▶ Read Hebrews 13:1-25

8. In verses 1-6, our author urges us to pursue love and godliness. Who should we love and how (v 1-3)?

> **DICTIONARY**
>
> **Forsake (v 5):** abandon.
> **Diverse (v 9):** varied.
> **Eternal (v 20):** everlasting.

• How else should we pursue godliness, and why (v 4-6)?

9. Verses 7 and 17 talk about Christian leaders. How does God use leaders in our lives?

• What should our attitude be toward them?

⊡ **explore more**

optional

Our author next encourages us once more that Jesus' covenant is better than the old covenant.

What comparison does he make in verses 11-12?

What does he urge us to do in response (v 13)?

10. We please God by faith in Jesus (11:6)—not by making animal sacrifices. But in verses 15-16 our author talks about two other kinds of sacrifice. What are they, and why are they expressions of faith?

⤇ apply

11. Our author's application boils down to these three commands: endure suffering and reproach (v 13), praise God (v 15), and do good (v 16). Which do you think is hardest? What specific things can you do to apply each of these commands in your own life?

⊡ getting personal

"Now may the God of peace who brought again from the dead our Lord Jesus, the great shepherd of the sheep, by the blood of the eternal covenant, equip you with everything good that you may do his will, working in us that which is pleasing in his sight" (v 20-21).

Where in your life do you particularly need God's help and equipping to do his will at the moment?

12. Think back over the whole of the time you have spent looking at the book of Hebrews. How would you sum up its message? If you had to choose one take-home point for your own life, what would it be?

⬆ pray

Hebrews 12 and 13 include a series of statements about God which should motivate us to put into practice the commands we are given, even when that is difficult. Look at 12:3, 7, and 28 and 13:6, 8, and 14 and use these verses to help you praise God.

Then use the words of 13:20-21 to help you to pray together.

An anchor
for the soul

Hebrews

LEADER'S GUIDE

Leader's Guide

INTRODUCTION

Leading a Bible study can be a bit like herding cats—everyone has a different idea of what the passage could be about, and a different line of enquiry that they want to pursue. But a good group leader is more than someone who just referees this kind of discussion. You will want to:

- correctly understand and handle the Bible passage. But also…

- encourage and train the people in your group to do this for themselves. Don't fall into the trap of spoon-feeding people by simply passing on the information in the Leader's Guide. Then…

- make sure that no Bible study is finished without everyone knowing how the passage is relevant for them. What changes do you all need to make in the light of the things you have been learning? And finally…

- encourage the group to turn all that has been learned and discussed into prayer.

Your Bible-study group is unique, and you are likely to know better than anyone the capabilities, backgrounds and circumstances of the people you are leading. That's why we've designed these guides with a number of optional features. If they're a quiet bunch, you might want to spend longer on *talkabout*. If your time is limited, you can choose to skip *explore more*, or get people to look at these questions at home. Can't get enough of Bible study? Well, some studies have optional extra homework projects. As leader, you can adapt and select the material to the needs of your particular group.

So what's in the Leader's Guide? The main thing that this Leader's Guide will help you to do is to understand the major teaching points in the passage you are studying, and how to apply them. As well as guidance for the questions, the Leader's Guide for each session contains the following important sections:

THE BIG IDEA

One or two key sentences will give you the main point of the session. This is what you should be aiming to have fixed in people's minds as they leave the Bible study. And it's the point you need to head back toward when the discussion goes off at a tangent.

SUMMARY

An overview of the passage, including plenty of useful historical background information.

OPTIONAL EXTRA

Usually this is an introductory activity that ties in with the main theme of the Bible study, and is designed to "break the ice" at the beginning of a session. Or it may be a "homework project" that people can tackle during the week.

So let's take a look at the various different features of a Good Book Guide:

⊕ talkabout

Each session kicks off with a discussion question, based on the group's opinions or experiences. It's designed to get people talking and thinking in a general way about the main subject of the Bible study.

⊡ investigate

The first thing you and your group need to know is what the Bible passage is about, which is the purpose of these questions. But watch out—people may come up with answers based on their experiences or teaching they have heard in the past, without referring to the passage at all. It's amazing how often we can get through a Bible study without actually looking at the Bible! If you're stuck for an answer, the Leader's Guide contains guidance for questions. These are the answers to direct your group to. This information isn't meant to be read out to people—ideally, you want them to discover these answers from the Bible for themselves. Sometimes there are optional follow-up questions (see ☒ in guidance for questions) to help you help your group get to the answer.

☺ explore more

These questions generally point people to other relevant parts of the Bible. They are useful for helping your group to see how the passage fits into the "big picture" of the whole Bible. These sections are OPTIONAL—only use them if you have time. Remember that it's better to finish in good time having really grasped one big thing from the passage, than to try and cram everything in.

➔ apply

We want to encourage you to spend more time working at application—too often, it is simply tacked on at the end. In the Good Book Guides, apply sections are mixed in with the investigate sections of the study. We hope that people will realize that application is not just an optional extra, but rather, the whole purpose of studying the

Bible. We do Bible study so that our lives can be changed by what we hear from God's word. If you skip the application, the Bible study hasn't achieved its purpose.

These questions draw out practical lessons that we can all learn from the Bible passage. You can review what has been learned so far, and think about practical differences that this should make in our churches and our lives. The group gets the opportunity to talk about what they personally have learned.

☺ getting personal

These can be done at home, but it is well worth allowing a few moments of quiet reflection during the study for each person to think and pray about specific changes they need to make in their own lives. Why not have a time for reporting back at the beginning of the following session, so that everyone can be encouraged and challenged by one another to make application a priority?

↑ pray

In Acts 4:25-30 the first Christians quoted Psalm 2 as they prayed in response to the persecution of the apostles by the Jewish religious leaders. Today however, it's not as common for Christians to base prayers on the truths of God's word as it once was. As a result, our prayers tend to be weak, superficial and self-centered rather than bold, visionary and God-centered.

The prayer section is based on what has been learned from the Bible passage. How different our prayer times would be if we were genuinely responding to what God has said to us through his word.

1

Hebrews 1:1-14
JESUS IN ALL HIS GLORY

THE BIG IDEA
Christ is supreme over all things. Our response should be simple: to give glory to God and to worship Christ.

SUMMARY
The author begins by showing that Christ is the fullest, final revelation of who God is (v 1-3). God has always been a speaking God. Formerly he spoke through the prophets, but now he has spoken ultimately through Jesus. That is because Jesus is God. He is the ruler and Creator of the world, he has the glory of God, and he is the exact representation of God. Jesus is the most glorious, most powerful person in the universe.

This means we should not be so easily impressed by the things of the world. In the remainder of the chapter, the author unveils how great and glorious Christ is by comparing him to angels—whom, it seems, the original audience of this letter had begun to honor and venerate.

The author proves the superiority of Jesus to angels using seven Old Testament quotations which all show the glory and superiority of Christ. He is the One who has a name above all other names, who is the only person worthy of worship, who lives forever, who rules all things, and by whom all things were made. It is Christ alone who should captivate our hearts.

OPTIONAL EXTRA
Write some famous names on pieces of paper and put them in a hat or bowl. Invite one person to pick a name. The rest of

the group must ask yes/no questions to figure out who the person on the piece of paper is. Once a few people have had a go, change the rules: this time they must do an impression of the person. Then play a third round: this time they are not allowed to speak but must act out who the person is. An optional fourth round can involve saying just one word to represent the name on the paper. You could finish by asking which is the best method of finding out who someone is. This is an icebreaker game which serves as an introduction to the idea of how we know what God is like.

GUIDANCE FOR QUESTIONS
1. Do you think people in our world today expect to hear from God? If they do, how do they think he will speak? Skeptics say that, if God exists at all, he isn't really a speaking God. He is distant and disengaged and no one can be sure what he's like. On the flip side, there are others who think God speaks through anything and everything: every religion, every spiritualist, every crystal ball—that there is no one channel that God speaks through primarily. But we'll see that the opening lines in the book of Hebrews refute both of these views.

2. The first two verses tell us twice that God has spoken. What are the differences between the way God spoke in verse 1 and the way he spoke in verse 2? The author breaks down all of history into two parts. In the past, God used to speak in certain ways; in the present, he speaks in a new way. For each of these there are three things to notice. When did he speak? To whom did he speak? And how did he speak?

- In verse 1, the first words are "Long ago." From the very start, God has been a speaking God. He made the world by speaking (Genesis 1:3-27)! He has been speaking for generations. "Our fathers" are believers that have come before us. The author has Israel in mind primarily. The most fundamental point, though, is how God spoke. He used to speak through chosen prophets who were God's mouthpieces to his people.
- In verse 2, the "last days" means the current time—beginning with Jesus' first coming and lasting till his second coming. God has spoken "to us." This is very personal. His word is for us today. The crescendo of these verses is that God no longer spoke through intermediaries but has shown up in person, speaking "by his Son." God came in the person of Christ and spoke to his people himself.

3. What do verses 2-3 tell us about the Son's power?

- Jesus is "appointed the heir of all things." The whole of creation belongs to him: he is its King.
- Jesus is the one "through whom also [God] created the world." He is the Creator. This is a way of saying he is God, because creation is something that only God does.
- Jesus "upholds the universe by the word of his power." This is another way to show that Jesus is God, because God is the one who sustains and upholds the world (see Psalm 104).

4. What do these verses tell us about how the Son reveals God?

- He is the one through whom God has spoken.

- He is "the radiance of the glory of God." The word "radiance" means "brightness" or "shining." In the Old Testament, God is often described as shining or bright. Jesus doesn't just reflect God's glory like Moses (see Exodus 34:29-35); he himself is the shining, bright, brilliant One.
- He is "the exact imprint of his nature." Jesus perfectly represents God's being. The word "imprint" could also be translated "stamp" and was often used to describe the impression of an image on a coin. It referred to the exact image of the king or emperor. The point is that if you have seen Jesus, you have seen God. After all, who can reveal God better than God?

5. What do these verses tell us about what the Son came to do? Jesus alone achieved a real, full, final purification from sins (v 3). We know this because he "sat down." That means his job was finished.

6. APPLY: We think of Jesus as our Savior from sin. But these verses remind us that he is also the sovereign King of everything. How will it change our lives if we remember this?

- We will stop taking Jesus for granted. Kings don't save their enemies; they destroy them. Yet here is the Lord who has given himself in order to purify us from our sins.
- We will become more prayerful because we recognize Jesus' power.
- We will be less anxious because we will entrust all our cares to Christ. (Of course, being fallen people, we would still worry; but this view of Jesus is the thing that will fight it.)
- We will be less despairing about the advance of the gospel, because we will remember that the great God who upholds the whole universe is the one

leading his army forward. Jesus is not going to lose: the world is his inheritance, and he will prevail in the end, however dark things seem.

7. What is the comparison in verse 4?

- Jesus is superior to angels. These are not the sweet little creatures we often think of. In the Bible, angels are amazing, glorious creatures of God, his attendants and special servants. Every time someone meets an angel, they are afraid.
- Jesus has a "more excellent" name than angels. This sums up what we have seen in the previous verses. Jesus is the Son of God: the name above all names. He has a status that no angel could come close to competing with.

8. In verses 5-6, how do we know that Jesus is better than angels? The writer's methodology is to use quotations from the Old Testament. He is saying that these passages are speaking about Jesus. In fact, the Old Testament is all about Jesus (Luke 24:44).

- Jesus is called God's Son (v 5). These are quotations from Psalm 2:7 (a psalm about God's promised King) and 2 Samuel 7:14 (God's promise to David about one of his descendants).
- Jesus is worshiped by angels (v 6). This is a quotation from the Greek translation of Deuteronomy 32:43.

EXPLORE MORE
Read Acts 13:32-33 and Romans 1:4. What, for Paul, is the key event that declares Jesus to be God's Son? The moment when Jesus was "declared to be the Son of God" (Romans 1:4) was his resurrection. This was when he ascended to his place of honor and glory. This is something the Roman world would have

understood. When sons came of age, they were formally bestowed with the family name, even though in one sense they had always had it. This is the best way to understand Jesus' sonship status. He "came of age" when he ascended into glory. This is why 2 Samuel 7:14 and Psalm 2:7 can say that "today", namely on the day of resurrection, Jesus was appointed as the Son.

9. What is the Son's role in verse 8?
Notice the throne language: Jesus is King. The author is citing Psalm 45:6. When he reads about God on his throne in the Old Testament, he sees that as applying to Christ.

10. What role do the angels have, meanwhile (v 7, 14)?

- v 7: The angels are Jesus' servants or "ministers" (v 7). This is a quote from Psalm 104.
- v 14: The author says the same thing: they are "ministering spirits" who "serve."

11. Re-read verses 7-14. How else do we see Jesus' superiority?

- v 8-9: Jesus is righteous above anyone else. This means that he has been anointed as a sign that he is greater than anyone else.
- v 10-12: This is a quote from Psalm 102, a psalm about creation. Jesus created everything, and that includes the angels. Jesus is eternal; he does not wear out like the world.
- v 13: Here the author cites Psalm 110:1. To be at the right hand of God is to be the one who has all God's authority and all his sovereign rule. It's a position of power. In fact, to be at the right hand of God is eventually to be the person who will come to conquer and judge the world. Notice the language here:

his enemies will be "a footstool for [his] feet." Jesus is not just a king but a warrior king—the one who will destroy all his enemies and set all things right.

12. APPLY: What do we tend to value the most—and how do those things compare to Jesus? How will this comparison change the way you think about or act toward those things?

Instead of being easily pleased with money, status, relationships, or anything else, we must keep looking to the glory of Christ. He is the one who has a name above all other names, who is the only person worthy of worship, who rules all things and by whom all things were made. It is Christ alone who should captivate our hearts.

2 Hebrews 2:1 – 3:6
A GREAT SALVATION

THE BIG IDEA
Jesus became human and died for us—not only to save us from sin but also to make us his children and bring us to glory. We must listen to this message!

SUMMARY
The author begins chapter 2 by giving us several reasons to pay attention to the message of the gospel (v 1-4)—warning us that if we do not, we risk drifting away.

Then we are told more about this message. The author explains how God became a man to save human beings. Jesus is the ultimate human—the perfect human—who is able to represent us before God.

To do this, the author first focuses on us as humans: who we are and what we were made to be and do (v 5-8). But in verse 8 we find out that humans have messed up and God's design is profoundly broken.

What we need is a perfect human to succeed where we have failed. So, in verse 9 our author shows how important it is that Christ became a real human being. He put himself

into our place. This means that he was able to deliver us from the problem we had got in to (v 10-18). He became a human, which meant he could represent humanity. He suffered and died on our behalf. We can be restored to the glory and honor that God intended, gaining a new identity as his children. And now Jesus continues to help us and represent us before God.

This message of salvation is truly "great"! It is far richer and deeper than we often think. So, 3:1-6 sums up by reminding us again who Christ is and who we are in him— encouraging us to respond to this message of salvation by fixing our eyes on Jesus.

OPTIONAL EXTRA
Start a group discussion about what the perfect human would be like. Start with more specific (and humorous!) questions such as "What would the perfect spouse/parent/boss/president be like?" Then ask what the perfect human would be like. What would he or she do and say—or not do and say? What qualities would they have? The point of these questions is firstly to see that all of us fall short

of perfection; and secondly to prepare the group to see that Jesus is the perfect human.

GUIDANCE FOR QUESTIONS

1. When in life do you have to pay attention? When are you good at doing so, and when is it more difficult? Why?
You may discuss school or university classes, meetings at work, church services, or family dynamics! Encourage the group to think about what makes it hard or easy to pay attention.

2. The author speaks about "a great salvation" in verse 3. What reasons does he give in verses 1-4 to pay attention to this message of salvation?
- Left to themselves, our hearts tend to "drift away" from God (v 1)
- It provides the way out from God's judgment. The author contrasts the "message declared by angels," the old covenant message which revealed God in types and shadows, with the "great salvation" of Jesus. During the time of the Old Testament, "every transgression or disobedience received a just retribution" (v 2). But Jesus offered himself to provide the way out from God's judgment.
- God holds us accountable for our response (v 2-3). If we reject the message of Jesus, which brings forgiveness, we will not escape judgment. We too will be held accountable for our sins.
- The message is trustworthy. It was declared by God himself through Jesus (v 3). We know about it because of the testimony of "those who heard" (v 3)— the eyewitnesses of Jesus' teachings, death, and resurrection. It has been authenticated by "signs and wonders" (v 4)—the miracles performed by Jesus, capped off by his resurrection. Finally, we know the gospel is true because we see

the Spirit at work in those who believe it (v 4).

3. Verse 6 talks about "man": the human race. What does the quotation in verses 6-8 tell us about humanity's place in the world?
- This is a quotation from Psalm 8. The psalm begins by reflecting on how small man seems, registering surprise that God would notice us (Hebrews 2:6). We are "lower than the angels" (2:7).
- Yet God has given us "glory and honor." That is, we are made to reflect his glory, because he has made us in his own image. He has made us for a special purpose.
- God also made human beings to be the guardians, protectors, and rulers of his world—with everything in subjection under us (v 8). Some day we will even have a role in ruling and judging angels (1 Corinthians 6:3).

4. In verse 8, God's plan for humanity seems to have gone wrong. Why do you think this is? In what ways are we ruled rather than being rulers? God designed everything to be under the dominion of human beings. Yet "we do not see everything in subjection to him."
The most significant thing that by nature rules every human is sin. We were designed to rule over angels, and yet it was an angelic being (Satan) who persuaded Adam and Eve to follow him and rebel against God. The result was that God's design for the world was profoundly broken. And it is not just that Adam sinned: his corruption has passed down to all humans after him. So, we are not ruling the world well and we are not reflecting God's glory well.

5. However, in verse 9, we see that this quotation is not just a description

of humanity but also of one particular human. **Who is it, and what has he done to make this psalm describe him so well?** It describes Jesus. He is the perfect human.

- He humbled himself to become a real human being, "lower than the angels."
- He was "crowned … with glory and honor" by being raised from the dead.

- **What is the result of that for us (v 9, 10)?**
  - v 9: Because Christ is the perfect human being, he can be our representative and "taste death for everyone."
  - v 10: This means that he brings us "to glory." Jesus was crowned with glory when he was raised from the dead. This is the future that awaits his followers, too. We will be raised up to the place of dignity that God always intended.

  NOTE: Verse 10 tells us that Jesus was made "perfect through suffering." This doesn't refer to the moral perfection of Jesus—he was always sinless—but to his effectiveness as our representative. He became human so that he could suffer and die on our behalf.

6. What is our identity now (v 11-13)?

This holiness makes us part of the same family—God's family. Jesus can call us "brothers" (v 12) and "the children God has given me" (v 13). These are quotations from Psalm 22:22 and Isaiah 8:18.

7. APPLY: This passage tells us that we were designed for glory but have fallen short of it. Discuss some of the limitations and problems that we experience as humans. What hope does this passage give us about how those things can be overcome?

There are many problems in the world. You may think for example of lack of education, racism, or economic inequality. But ordinary humans cannot be the ultimate solution. Education, government programs, and cultural change are not enough. This is because we are the real problem with the world.

At the same time, we need to recognize the distinctive glory and dignity of humans. Every person you run into is a little immortal, made in the image of God. Humans have a distinctive purpose to reflect God's glory and rule his world.

Only through Christ can we be restored to the glory and honor that God intended. Because Christ is the perfect human being, he can deliver us from the problem we have got ourselves into. In him, God promises to make us into the kind of humanity he originally designed.

8. According to verses 14-16, why did Jesus become human?

Jesus became "flesh and blood" because he was out to help flesh and blood. This is explained in verse 16. Did Jesus set out on a plan to save angels? No. He set out on a plan to save you and me—"the offspring of Abraham." (In the New Testament, this refers to all who have faith in Christ. See Galatians 3:29.) Jesus became a human so that he could die as a human. The ultimate purpose was to destroy the devil and free us from death.

9. What do the following things mean, and what difference do they make to our lives now?

- **Jesus destroyed the one who has the power of death (v 14).** Saying that Satan "has the power of death" doesn't mean that he really controls death. God is the one who gives life and takes it away (1 Samuel 2:6). No, Satan has the power of death in the sense that he influences the thing that causes death: sin. Jesus' death sets us free not only from sin and death but also from the "fear of death" which had us in "lifelong slavery" (v 15). This should radically change our lives. You can really live for Christ if you know that death has no power over you. We spend so much time thinking about how long we are going to live and planning for the time we have left. But in Christ, we live eternally. We need to get the fear of death off our shoulders and live like we are going to live forever!

- **Jesus made propitiation for sins (v 17).** This means he satisfied God's anger against sin. Jesus is like a sponge which soaks up all the wrath of God so that there is no more left. God is right to be angry at sin, but if you trust in Jesus, there is no anger left for you. God's favor now rests on you and you do not need to be afraid.

- **Jesus suffered when tempted (v 18).** You may be able to think of many different examples of Jesus' suffering. He was also tempted in all the ways we are tempted. The temptation of personal glory (Luke 4:9-12). The temptation of wealth and power (Luke 4:5-8). Perhaps the greatest temptation Jesus experienced was in the Garden of Gethsemane, when he said, "Remove this cup from me" (Luke 22:42). He was tempted to do anything he could to avoid suffering. Jesus never gave into temptation, but that doesn't mean he did not feel it.

According to verse 17, this makes him "merciful" (compassionate toward us, because he knows what it is like to be in difficult situations) and "faithful" (because if he endured temptation and suffering, then he is able to be always there for you, always praying for you). We can be confident that Jesus understands us, loves us, and is acting as our good representative before God.

10. What does the author tell us to do in response to all we've heard so far (3:1, 6)?

- v 1: "Consider Jesus." The NIV translates this "Fix your thoughts on Jesus." We fix our thoughts on just about anything sometimes—anything we think might satisfy us more than Jesus. But the author is telling us not to get distracted.

- v 6: "Hold fast our confidence and our boasting in our hope." This hope is the "great salvation" outlined in chapter 2: that Jesus came as God enfleshed to bring forgiveness of sins, and that he has defeated death and will bring us to glory with himself.

11. To encourage us to do this, what does the author tell us about…
- **our identity (v 1, 6)?**

  - The author calls us "holy" (v 1). This means that we have the Spirit in us and have been set apart for God's purposes. He is at work within us. This encourages us to run from sin, because it is entirely against who we are.

  - He also calls us "brothers." We have a new family. This highlights the significance of church, which is an incredibly powerful tool that God uses to remind us that we belong in his family.

  - He says that we "share in a heavenly calling" (v 1). We are called toward a heavenly destination. We belong with Jesus; that is who we are. Therefore, we should seek to represent him well.

  - In verse 6 the author says that we are "God's house." A Jewish reader might have assumed the author is talking about the Old Testament temple. But the house that God is building through Jesus is not a physical structure; it is the people of God. Ephesians 2:22 tells us that this means we are "a dwelling place for God." The Spirit of Christ lives in his body, the church. And the Spirit helps us to fix our thoughts on him.

- **Jesus' identity?**
  - "Apostle" (v 1) means "sent." Jesus was sent by God to speak for God to humans. A "high priest" (v 1) goes in the opposite direction. He represents humans to God. Jesus, uniquely, goes both ways. He can do this because he is both God and man. He perfectly bridges the gap between humans and God.
  - The author compares Jesus to Moses. Both are faithful servants of God (v 2), but Christ is more glorious (v 3). Moses was a major figure in the Jewish faith: the one who delivered the law and set up the whole system of temple worship. But our author is saying that Christ is the one who fulfills all that Moses pointed toward ("the things that were to be spoken later," v 5). He is greater than Moses, just as he is greater than angels.

EXPLORE MORE
What is the comparison in verse 3? Jesus and Moses are compared to a builder and a house. Moses was only part of the house, while Christ built the house. This means that Christ has more honor.
What does that tell us about who Jesus is (v 4)? Jesus is the Creator and builder of the people of God because he is God. "The builder of all things is God."
The imagery changes in verses 5-6. How do Moses and Jesus relate to the house now? Moses is a servant in the house, but Christ is the Son and heir. Again, this means that Christ deserves more honor than Moses. This may seem obvious to us, but it was hugely significant to a first-century Jewish audience. Moses was one of the founding figures of God's people. Saying

that Jesus is more important than Moses was like saying that a modern local politician is more important than George Washington. It seemed crazy! The author's point is that Jesus is not just some recent human figure. He has been "over God's house" since the beginning. We must not underestimate Jesus' power and glory.

12. APPLY: The author tells us to "pay much closer attention to what we have heard" (2:1), to "consider Jesus" (3:1), and to "hold fast our confidence and our boasting in our hope" (3:6). How can you put these things into practice this week?

- The warning in 2:1-3 should spur us on and make us examine ourselves. We need to regularly repent of sin and ask for God's help in paying attention to him.
- In our world today, the spirit of individualism reigns supreme. But we are God's family (2:11-13; 3:1) and God's house (3:6) together. That means it is vital to be committed to one another and linked together as his people. When we spend time with other Christians, we help one another to fix our eyes on Jesus. This is partly because we are being taught the word in community. It is also because we are reassured when we see the Spirit at work in God's people around us (2:4).
- Your group may also come up with more specific ideas of how they could pay closer attention to God's message this week. For some it may be learning a particular verse or verses from the passage in this study. For others it may be committing to a regular Bible-reading slot. For others it may be seeking to "boast" more about the message of salvation to their unbelieving friends or family.

13. APPLY: How does this passage enlarge your understanding of salvation? What do you feel most excited about?

- Jesus doesn't just save us from sin (2:17). He also died so that we don't have to die (v 9). He brings us to glory (v 10) and makes us holy (v 11). He calls us brothers and makes us children of God (v 11-14). He destroyed the devil and released us from slavery (v 15). He continues to help us (v 18). And he has made us his house and dwelling place (3:6).

- Encourage the group to reflect on what each of these things means for us today. What is each person most thankful for here, and what difference does it make to them? We should all be deeply thankful and excited for what Jesus has done. And we should be desperate to tell others about this wonderful message!

3

Hebrews 3:7 – 4:13

IF YOU HEAR HIS VOICE

THE BIG IDEA

Looking back to the wilderness generation of Israelites teaches us a key lesson: don't fall into unbelief! God has promised us an ultimate rest; we can enter it by believing in his word.

SUMMARY

Our passage opens with a warning not to make the same mistake as the wilderness generation (3:7-19). God had promised to take them to the promised land and give them rest. But because of their rebellion and unbelief, that generation did not make it.

The author then makes a remarkable statement: "The promise of entering his rest still stands" (4:1). The rest which God offered to the Israelites is still available to us today. This is because the ultimate rest God had in mind was not the promised land after all. We know this because God renewed his promise of rest long after the Israelites entered the promised land. (This renewed promise was made in Psalm 95, which our author quotes throughout this passage.)

What "rest" really means is not any physical plot of land but the eternal, heavenly rest which God himself enjoys (v 1-11). We enter this rest by faith. In one sense, we already entered it when we first believed in Christ. But the overall thrust of the passage is forward looking. Our ultimate rest is yet to come. One day we will rest from the trials and tribulations of life. Our journey will be over and we will be in our true home: the real promised land of heaven.

Verse 11 urges us to "strive to enter that rest." We must listen to God and obey his word, not fall away in rebellion like the Israelites. Verses 12-13 explain why we should listen to God: because his word is living, active, and powerful. It is always trustworthy and true.

OPTIONAL EXTRA

Ask a few group members to come ready

to share a particular Bible verse or passage that has spoken to them in a significant way. How did God use his word to speak to them, and what impact did it have on their lives? You could share these as an ice-breaker at the start, or at the end before you pray together.

GUIDANCE FOR QUESTIONS

1. How do you respond when someone doesn't really listen to you? How about when someone does listen but doesn't take what you say seriously? Today's passage speaks repeatedly about hearing, listening to, and believing God's voice and God's word. These questions are designed to introduce these themes.

2. Our passage begins with a quotation (from Psalm 95:7-11). Which phrase is the key warning here? "Do not harden your hearts" (v 8). This warning is also repeated in verse 15.

3. The warning involves a comparison with the generation of Israelites whom God brought out of Egypt. What did these people do (v 9, 16-18)? They "put [God] to the test" despite having seen God's works (v 9). In other words, they "heard and yet rebelled" (v 16); they sinned (v 17) and were disobedient (v 18).

• **What was the root cause of this (v 19)?** It was "because of unbelief."

EXPLORE MORE

Read Numbers 13:25 – 14:11.
Why don't the people want to enter the land? The spies come back with scary descriptions of the powerful inhabitants of the promised land. So, the people are too afraid to enter it.
What do Joshua and Caleb say the people are doing? They are rebelling against God because they fear the people of the land instead of trusting God's protection (14:9).
What does God say about it? God gives the same diagnosis but puts it more strongly. The people "despise" him and disbelieve him (v 11).

4. How did God respond (v 11, 19)? He told them that they would be unable to enter his "rest." The people were on the very edge of the promised land, but most would never get there. You can read what God said to them in full in Numbers 14:26-35.

5. How does the author apply this story to his readers (v 12-15)? With this story of Israel's rebellion as the backdrop, the author issues a clear warning to readers. We need to be careful not to fall away.
We know from other passages in the Bible that a genuine believer cannot lose their salvation (e.g. John 10:28). But we need to take this warning seriously. When it comes to who is saved, God has a habit of breaking our expectations. There are some who have every reason to believe and yet they don't (e.g. Judas, one of Jesus' own disciples). And there are some who we think will never believe and yet they do (e.g. Paul, a hater of Christians). This reminds us that salvation is in the Lord's hands: "I will have mercy on whom I have mercy" (Romans 9:15).
This warning also teaches us that a good start does not guarantee a good finish. The real test is whether a person demonstrates perseverance—whether "we hold our original confidence firm to the end" (v 14). This is what the wilderness generation failed to do, despite having seen so much evidence of God's miracles and divine presence.

6. APPLY: What does the author tell us to do in order to avoid falling into unbelief and sin? "Exhort one another every day" (v 13).

- **How can you put this into practice?**
  - We should be regularly exhorting one another to press on and not drift away. We often fail to urge one another on in faith—perhaps because we feel that another person's faith is not our business, or we fear they will take offense. But accountability is a great ally in the war against apostasy. We all need it.
  - It can be helpful to have an "accountability partner": choose a trusted friend, ask them to intervene if they ever see you drifting away or falling into sin, and promise to do the same for them. This is especially important if you are facing a specific temptation or a time of particular suffering or uncertainty.
  - We can also encourage friends regularly by sending them Bible verses or asking how we can pray for them. Why not aim to send a message to someone every time you read the Bible, telling them briefly what God has been teaching you? This can be a way of encouraging another person to press on even if you are not explicitly warning them away from sin.

7. God's people did eventually make it to the promised land, led by Joshua. But how do verses 7-8 show that this did not fulfil God's ultimate promise of rest? Joshua was famous for leading God's people into the physical land of Canaan. But he did not lead them to the ultimate rest God had in mind. Instead God made the promise of rest again, "through David" (v 7; that is, in the psalm quoted throughout this passage). In Psalm 95, written "long afterward," God gave his people a renewed invitation to hear his voice, believe in him, and thereby enter his rest.

8. What is God's true rest like (v 3-4, 9-10)? It is like joining God in his heavenly Sabbath. Verses 3-4 remind us of the creation account, when God rested on the seventh day. Ever since then, God has enjoyed a perpetual, eternal "Sabbath" in heaven. This doesn't mean God is inactive—he is busy in all sorts of ways (John 5:17)—but he is still resting from his work of creation. And those who believe in Jesus get to join God in this eternal Sabbath rest (Hebrews 4:9). Our labors will finally come to an end.

As soon as we believe in Christ and the Spirit dwells within us, we can enjoy a dimension of rest even in the present. And yet the overall thrust of the entire passage is forward looking. Our ultimate rest is still yet to come. We still long for, and strive for, the ultimate rest that awaits us in heaven—our real promised land.

9. How do we enter it (v 1-3, 11)?
- We need fear (v 1). In other words, we need to take seriously the danger of neglecting this great offer of salvation.
- We need faith (v 2-3). Israel's lack of faith is a sober reminder that we must do more than merely hear the word. We need to believe it. It is easy to think that faith is a meritorious act, something you build up strength to do and feel proud of yourself for doing. But in fact, faith is just grabbing hold of the thing that saves us—namely, Jesus. What matters is not just faith itself, but the object of our faith. What saves us is Jesus; faith is the way we get Jesus.
- We need to fight (v 11). The word "strive" reminds us that effort, diligence, and perseverance are essential to the Christian life. We are not saved by

our efforts—we are only saved by the grace of Christ. But the Christian life still involves effort! It is not passive or detached but active and intentional.

10. What do you think it means that God's word is…

- **"living"?** This means that a living person is revealed in it. Since God's word is empowered by the Holy Spirit, when we encounter the word we encounter God. When the content of the message and the words themselves take root in our hearts, God is meeting his people. This is the stunning difference between the Bible and every other book in the world.

- **"active"?** God's word doesn't just say things; it does things. It is busy working, changing, building, convicting, encouraging, exposing, rebuking, giving light and wisdom, carving out the path of our lives, and showing us the truth of God. It can help you with any problem in your life. It equips you for every good work.

- **"sharper than any two-edged sword"?** God's word is made to penetrate the human heart. The word of God is not just a way to get to know God but also a way to get to know yourself. When you read the Bible and let it penetrate your heart, you will be "exposed." The word of God will show you who you really are and what your real problems are. It will get into your heart and heal it.

11. Do you think this is supposed to be scary or encouraging? Don't miss the sober warning here. If you don't deal with those things in your heart that are tripping you up, then you might find yourself like the Israelites—doubting, disbelieving and turning away from the living God. And when the word does surgery on our souls,

it may be painful. At the same time, these verses reveal that God's word is completely trustworthy. In it and through it, God is personally present and powerfully acts. We may be exposed, but we are exposed to one who loves us and is inviting us into his heavenly rest. We can trust him!

12. APPLY: "Today, if you hear his voice, do not harden your hearts." What implications does this have for the way we approach the Bible? God has manifested himself in his word. That is the primary way of meeting and interacting with him. It is the way he speaks to us. This means that:

- Any encounter with the Bible is a serious matter. When we read the word, we are encountering the Lord of the universe— and that is a sobering thing to consider. Studying the Bible is not to be taken lightly.

- The Bible is not just a book filled with helpful information. We should expect to hear God speak to us through it.

- We should put what the Bible says ahead of what our own personal experiences teach us. It is authoritative.

We have an opportunity "every day, as long as it is called 'today'" (3:13), to hear from God. We should therefore persevere in reading the Bible regularly.

We should also persevere in obedience. "Hardening your heart" means choosing to disobey what you have heard. It is vital that we not only hear the word but obey it. When we read the Bible, we should ask ourselves what God is calling us to do or not to do, and then act upon that.

Hebrews 4:14 – 6:12
4 HOLDING FAST

THE BIG IDEA
Because Jesus is greater than any earthly priest, we can draw near to God with confidence—but those who fall away will be subject to judgment. So, we must persevere in faith and strive for spiritual growth.

SUMMARY
The author now shows us what we need in order to go before the throne of God confidently (4:14 – 5:10). He develops the theme of Christ as high priest. The ancient Israelites had earthly high priests who went before God on behalf of the people, making sacrifices for sin. But Jesus is better than these priests.

Like an earthly high priest, Jesus is a human, which means that he can relate to us. He has experienced everything in this life that is dark and difficult and problematic. So, he is the one we can come to for sympathy and compassion. But unlike any other human, Christ has no sins of his own. This means that he can fully purify us from sin—unlike any earthly high priest. Jesus speaks for us, acts for us, intercedes for us, and represents us. We can now have confidence before God.

The author will go into more detail about Jesus' priesthood later in his letter. But he now pauses to give his readers another warning. They are like spiritual toddlers (5:11-14) and so he fears they may fall away altogether (6:1-8). But he finishes with a sense of optimism (6:9-12): he lists some ways in which they are bearing fruit, and encourages them to strive for spiritual growth.

The second half of this passage may seem like a detour. But it fits with the encouragement to hold fast which comes at the start (4:14). If we fall away and reject Christ's salvation, we will be subject to judgment. We must continue to draw near to the throne of grace.

OPTIONAL EXTRA
Prepare some examples of people you admire for their perseverance—or ask group members in advance to think of their own. These might be athletes, businesspeople, artists, or your own friends and family. How has each person shown perseverance? Why is that perseverance worthwhile?

GUIDANCE FOR QUESTIONS
1. If someone said to you, "I feel totally confident before God," how would you respond? A good way to respond would be to say, "Why?" What is their confidence based on? By nature, all of us are in a precarious position as we stand before the holy court of God. We are sinful and he is holy. We cannot stand before him on our own merits. So, if someone thinks that God is lucky to have them on his team, they are wrong! You need to help them to see why that's the case. However, we can be confident before God if we are in Christ. Because of what he has done, we can walk into God's presence with complete assurance that he loves us. If that's why someone is confident before God, rejoice with them! This could be a helpful question to return to at the end of the study. How does the group's answer change after they have read this passage?

2. What did a priest in Old Testament Israel do, and why was it important that they were human (5:1-2)? A priest went before God on behalf of the people (v 1). By nature, the people were sinful and could not come near to God. Yet God dwelt in their midst (in the temple)! This was made possible by the work of priests, who were like go-betweens. They dealt with the problem of sin by making sacrifices and teaching the people God's law. (We will look in much more detail at the sacrificial system in Study 6.)

It was important that they were "chosen from among men" because it meant they experienced life like everyone else: the fallenness of the world, the problems, the temptations, the weaknesses and so on. This enabled them to "deal gently with the ignorant and wayward" (v 2). When people fell into sin, the priests' job was to help them.

3. How is Jesus similar (4:15)? What events in Jesus' life do you think the author could be referring to?
- He sympathizes with our weaknesses. Jesus did not shield himself from the fallenness of the world. He was "despised and rejected by men, a man of sorrows and acquainted with grief" (Isaiah 53:3). He really did experience everything in this life that is dark and difficult and problematic, from physical suffering to relational troubles. And when he hung on the cross he was not only scorned by all around him, but drank from the cup of his Father's wrath poured out on him in the place of sinners.
- He has been tempted as we are. He was tempted by Satan in the wilderness: tempted by wealth, by power, by comfort. He was tempted in the garden of Gethsemane to avoid suffering. Whatever

you are tempted by, Jesus can relate to you in this way as well.

- **In 5:7, how does the author illustrate this? How do you think he wants you to feel when you read this verse?** The author is likely referring to Jesus' cries to his Father in the garden of Gethsemane (Luke 22:41-44). So much did he dread what was coming—the wrath of his own Father—that his sweat was like drops of blood. The language here is emotive: the author wants to drive home the point that Jesus' suffering was very, very real. This may make us feel grateful for what Jesus willingly went through on our behalf. Or, if we have also offered up "loud cries and tears" to God in prayer, these words will comfort us: Jesus really does know how we feel.

4. What is the key difference between Jesus and the priests in Old Testament Israel (4:15; 5:3; 5:8-9)? The disadvantage of the priests' weaknesses was that it meant they sinned too. Therefore, when they made offerings, they did not just make them on behalf of the people. They had to make offerings on their own behalf (5:3). But Jesus is "without sin" (4:15). For this reason, he surpasses the Old Testament priests.
NOTE: The language in verse 8 raises a natural question. How is it that Jesus "learned" obedience? Wasn't he always perfect? Yes, he was always perfect. But to say Jesus learned obedience is not to suggest he was at one time disobedient. Rather it emphasizes Jesus' experience as a human being who learned what it was like to obey God even in the midst of great suffering.

- **What does this mean for us?** Jesus can relate, but he can also save. Because he is perfect, he brings "eternal salvation" (5:9). (We will find out more about why Jesus' perfection means he can bring salvation in Study 6.)

5. How should we respond (4:14-16)?

• We should "hold fast our confession" (v 14). Do not abandon what you believe about Jesus, because there is no better place to turn than this intercessor. He alone can provide mercy and grace (v 16).

• This means we can "draw near" to God's throne (v 16). We couldn't stand before God on our own merits. But we have eternal security in heaven because Jesus is representing us. When God looks at us, he sees the perfect purity and righteousness of his Son surrounding us. This means you can march right into the throne room of God, saying, "I am God's child. Jesus has saved me."

6. APPLY: How does this passage help us…

• **in times of particular suffering and weakness?** Jesus' example in 5:7 is a good one to follow when we are suffering. We can, like him, ask the Father to relieve us and comfort us. But whether the answer is yes or no, we must remain obedient to God—acting with "reverence." And—praise God—we can remember that we have a great high priest who is able to sympathize with our weaknesses. We can, with confidence, draw near to him in prayer, asking for mercy and grace to help us in our need.

• **when we are tempted by sin?** It is comforting to know that Jesus can relate to us in temptation. He sympathizes and wants to help us avoid sin. It may be helpful to look up Matthew 4:1-11 to find out how Jesus dealt with temptation. Also remember that Jesus has given us his Holy Spirit to help us become holy and righteous. When we ask God for help in temptation, he always hears us.

If you do fall into sin, remember that if you are Jesus' follower, he will never, ever stop loving you, pleading your case, and representing you before God. By your faith in Jesus, God views you as a pure person. You can still have confidence to come before him.

• **when we long for a sympathetic friend?** Christ is the one we should come to for sympathy and compassion. If we have drunk deeply of the compassion available to us in Christ, then we no longer have to find ways to get it from others. Go to Christ, who fully sympathizes with your weaknesses, and then you can serve others by showing them the very sympathy and compassion that was shown to you.

7. In 5:11-14, the author says his readers are like spiritual toddlers! What does it mean that they are living on "milk"?

• They don't listen. They are "dull of hearing" (v 11) and have to be taught the same thing again and again (v 12). This is a sign of selfishness—they "ought to be teachers" by now, but instead they have become only takers in the church, and not givers.

• They are "unskilled in the word of righteousness" (v 13). They have not learned how to rightly understand the word of God. They have not grown in their knowledge of the word of God.

• **Why is it so important to grow in maturity and go onto "solid food" instead?** The mature are those who are "trained … to distinguish good from evil" (v 14). If you are an immature Christian, you cannot always separate right from wrong, and you are susceptible to deception—like a toddler who runs out into the street, unaware of the danger.

If you are not growing up in your faith, you are more likely to be tricked by those who want to take you down wrong paths.

8. If we believe in Jesus but then fall away, what is the result (6:4-6)? Restoration is impossible (v 6). This is difficult and even frightening. However, there is hope. When we see someone leaving the covenant community, we don't know for certain that they have fallen away for good. Some people have periods of rebellion and resistance, and church discipline can bring them back in. We should always hope that that could happen when someone seems to be leaving the faith.

EXPLORE MORE
Read Matthew 7:21-22.
In this passage, how could you appear to be a true follower of Christ without really being one? Here, Jesus describes people who think they are Christians because they call on his name and even perform miracles. But they are not really his followers. They never sought to do God's will.
What are the similarities between the person described in Matthew 7:21-22 and the person described in Hebrews 6:4-6?
• They are "enlightened" (Hebrews 6:4). This means they have received and understood the truth that Jesus is Lord.
• They have experienced spiritual privileges— "tasted the heavenly gift," "shared in the Holy Spirit" (v 4), and known "the powers of the age to come" (v 5). This may mean benefiting from the spiritual gifts of others or seeing powerful signs and wonders. It is also possible for non-Christians to exhibit spiritual giftedness—as the people Jesus described did. God's Spirit can work through people even when he does not dwell in them for salvation.

• Yet they have still "fallen away" (v 6). They are not doing God's will. By rejecting God, they are basically crucifying Christ again!
How can we make sure we are not this kind of person? We need to seek God's will above all else (Matthew 7:21). Remember the lesson of the wilderness generation in Hebrews 4: they failed to enter God's rest because of disobedience. True faith in Christ means obeying his word. This theme becomes clearer in the rest of this study.

9. In the analogy in Hebrews 6:7-9, what is the equivalent of receiving but then rejecting Jesus? A person receiving the good news about Jesus is like a land soaking up rain. If they reject Jesus and fall into sin, they are producing thistles instead of good crops. This kind of land is "worthless" and "to be burned" (v 8).

• **What is the author warning us that we should and should not do?** This warning is a reminder to each of us to make sure that we own our faith for ourselves. We must make sure we are growing and producing good crops, not treating Jesus' offer of salvation ungratefully like land that responds to rain by producing thistles.

10. What "good crops" does the author describe in verses 9-12? Despite being worried about their immaturity, the author does see some things that make him think that falling away will not be the fate of his readers. There are three areas of fruitfulness he mentions in verse 10: their labors in ministry ("your work"), their affection for God ("the love that you have shown for his name"), and their love for God's people ("serving the saints"). We can treat these three things as a litmus test for whether we are really saved, because together they express what it means to be Christlike; and any Christian, no matter how long they have been a Christian, can participate in them at some level.

11. What advice does he give for how to press ahead?

- We must be serious about our faith—showing "earnestness" (v 11).
- We must be hardworking, not "sluggish" (v 12). We cannot work our way to heaven, but the Christian life still involves labor. There is energy and hard work involved.
- We must have "patience" (v 12). Someday, we are going to inherit the promises that the book of Hebrews talks about; but it will not happen overnight. It's a long haul. We need to persevere in our faith.

12. APPLY: Practically speaking, how can we find a balance between being confident in our standing before God (4:16) and yet continuing to strive for growth (6:1, 12)?

- Do an assessment of your own Christian growth occasionally. Ask: If I look back at myself five years ago, is there any difference now? Am I moving closer to God and not further from him? Am I growing in the fruit of the Spirit (Galatians 5:22-23)? Am I helping others to learn the truth?
- Be a reader and keep getting to know God's word better. We should always be growing in the knowledge of God.
- Remember that no spiritual privileges are the basis for salvation. Whatever you have experienced or learned in your life, keep coming back to the fact that you are saved through faith alone, in Christ alone.

5 Hebrews 6:13 – 7:28
A SURE AND STEADFAST ANCHOR

THE BIG IDEA

Jesus is an anchor for our souls because as a priest "after the order of Melchizedek," he represents us eternally before God, giving us total security.

SUMMARY

In the Christian life, you are going to get beaten around by waves. What you need more than anything is an anchor. And we have one.

In Hebrews 6:13-19 our author uses the example of Abraham, the founding father of God's people. God promised Abraham a son (and ultimately many descendants). Although Abraham and his wife Sarah were too old to have children, God fulfilled his promise. This example assures us that we can trust what God has promised to us.

6:20 leads us into chapter 7, where we see why Jesus is the greatest reason to trust God.

7:1-10 introduces the figure of Melchizedek. We meet Melchizedek in Genesis 14:17-24, when he greets Abraham after a battle. The story suggests that Melchizedek was superior to Abraham. This is partly because of the way Melchizedek is described. It is also because he blessed Abraham and Abraham gave him a tenth of everything he had won in the battle.

Most Old Testament priests were descendants of Abraham (specifically, descendants of Levi, who was one of Abraham's great-grandsons—so they are called "Levitical" priests). But Melchizedek was a priest of a different kind. Since Melchizedek was superior to Abraham, his priesthood was also superior to the priesthood of Levi.

That matters because Christ is "after the order of Melchizedek." In Psalm 110, God promised to continue the priesthood of Melchizedek (Hebrews 7:11-22). Jesus is the fulfillment of that promise—which means he is superior to any other priest.

7:23-28 expands on why Jesus' priesthood is so much better: he represents us to God eternally rather than passing away, and he is perfectly sinless. This means that we can have great confidence that our sins have been forgiven. This is our anchor, keeping us secure when we are doubting or struggling with sin. We can draw near to God through Jesus with confidence.

OPTIONAL EXTRA

Split the group into two, ideally in two separate rooms. Each group draws up a list of charades. They send a representative to the other group to act out each charade. When the other group has guessed it correctly, the representative returns to their own group and ticks it off the list. A new representative goes to the other group to act out the next word. At the end, which representative was most effective?

GUIDANCE FOR QUESTIONS

1. What things make it difficult to trust God and his promises? It might be pain in your life or others' lives, or terrible news stories, or hostility from unbelievers, or intellectual objections, or something else.

• **What "anchors" keep your faith strong in times of doubt?** Encourage the group to share practical ideas of how they remain steadfast in faith. Ultimately (as our passage today will show), we can trust God because of Jesus.

2. God promised to give Abraham many descendants. Why did Abraham know he could trust this promise (6:13-18)?
• God swore "by himself" (v 13). He is the very highest authority to swear on.
• God's oath "guaranteed" his promise (v 17). God did not need to swear an oath. His promises are always true. But he swore an oath to Abraham in order to help and reassure him. (Read God's oath in Genesis 22:16-17.)
• God's purposes are "unchangeable" (v 17).
• It is "impossible" for God to lie (v 18).

3. How is this promise relevant to us?
• Abraham is a good example of trusting God when it is hard to do so. When the author says he "patiently waited," he means that Abraham waited until he and his wife were both old—too old to have children! But God gave them the child he had promised anyway. When we are doubting, Abraham's example will help us.
• God's promise was not just to Abraham. He also wanted to convince "the heirs of the promise" (v 17). As surprising as it may be, the oath that God swore to Abraham

is for all Christians. In Christ, we are part of God's promise to bless the nations through Abraham's family.

EXPLORE MORE
Read Romans 4:11-12, 16-18.
God fulfilled his promise not only with physical descendants but with spiritual ones. Who is Abraham the "father" of? Those who walk in faith. Abraham's physical descendants were circumcised—but Paul tells us that faith is what makes us Abraham's true heirs, whether we are circumcised or not. If we have faith that God can do what he promised (Romans 4:21), we become heirs of Abraham, blessed and made righteous by God.

4. What is the other reason to trust God here (Hebrews 6:19-20)? Jesus. He has gone "behind the curtain" (v 19). The curtain blocked off the Holy of Holies, the part of the temple in Jerusalem where God's presence dwelt. But Jesus has gone into God's presence on our behalf as our high priest. This is for us "a sure and steadfast anchor of the soul."

5. How is Melchizedek described in 7:1-3? In what ways is he similar to Jesus?
- v 1: Melchizedek was the king of Salem—which would later become Jerusalem. He was also a priest of God (v 1). No other figure in Israel was ever both king and priest—until Jesus.
- v 2: The name "Melchizedek" literally means "king of righteousness." "Salem" means "peace," so he is also a king of peace. Both phrases describe Jesus (see Isaiah 9:6; 11:4).
- v 3: He seemed eternal. Of course, Melchizedek was a normal human. But the way that he is presented in Scripture (in Genesis 14:8-16) makes it seem like he has

no beginning or end. This means that he resembles "the Son of God."

6. Abraham tithed (gave a tenth of what he had won in a battle) to Melchizedek. How does this prove the superiority of Melchizedek's priesthood (v 4-6, 9-10)?
- v 4: Abraham (who was a great "patriarch" or founding father) would only have given spoils to someone who was also truly great.
- v 5-6: Normally the Levitical priests were given tithes—a tenth of income—from everybody who came to worship. But with Melchizedek, tithes are being paid to someone who is not a Levite or a descendant of Abraham.
- v 9-10: If Melchizedek received tithes from Abraham, he must be superior to Abraham. That means he must be superior to the Levites. Our author explains this by saying that Levi was "still in the loins of" Abraham. The point is that Levi is a descendant of Abraham and therefore cannot be greater than him. Effectively, he was paying tithes to Melchizedek too! The chain of superiority must go like this: Melchizedek > Abraham > Levi > all Levitical priests.

- **What other proofs are given for Melchizedek's superiority (v 6-8)?**
  - Melchizedek blessed Abraham—which means he must be greater (v 6-7).
  - Melchizedek's priesthood is eternal: Abraham's tithes are not received by "mortal men" but by "one of whom it is testified that he lives" (v 8).

7. APPLY: When you are doubting or uncertain, how does it help to remember that Jesus is a priest similar to Melchizedek? Encourage the group to think specifically about the scenarios they outlined in Q1 and come up with practical ideas of what they could do to help themselves to trust God.

- Jesus is the king of righteousness and peace. When we are uncertain about what to do, we can ask him to guide us into righteousness. When we are feeling overwhelmed or attacked, we can ask him to provide peace. We can trust him with any problem.

- Jesus is eternal. This means he lives forever to represent us to God. When we doubt our salvation, we can look to Jesus and know that we are eternally secure.

- Even if you are full of doubts, you can trust the truth of who God is and what Jesus has done. Most importantly, when the storms come, instead of looking around at our problems or inward at ourselves, we need to look forward to the day when we will be with Christ.

8. Why was a different priesthood needed (v 11, 18-19)?

- The Levitical priesthood was unable to attain "perfection" (v 11, 19). In other words, it was unable to really cleanse God's people from their sins and make them fit to dwell with God forever.

- Jesus allows us to really "draw near to God" (v 19)—something the old priesthood could never do.

9. How do we know that Jesus is in "the order of Melchizedek" (v 13-17)?

- He comes from the tribe of Judah (v 13-14), the tribe of kings. This means that he can be both priest and king at the same time—like Melchizedek.

- He has become a priest "by the power of an indestructible life" (v 16)—like Melchizedek, who seemed eternal. Our author provides proof for this point in verse 17 by citing from Psalm 110:4.

10. How do we know that we can rely on this priesthood (v 20-22)? God swore an oath. The author cites a new portion of Psalm 110:4 to prove this. God swore an oath to give us an extra degree of assurance: Christ's priesthood is certain. This oath makes Jesus the "guarantor" of a better covenant—a better way of relating to God. Jesus will always be there, interceding for us.

11. What are the key differences between Jesus and the Levitical priests, and why are these differences so important for us (v 23-28)?

- v 23-25: Every Levitical priest was temporary, but Christ's priesthood is eternal. This means we can have eternal security. His intercession for us will never end and we can be certain of our salvation.

- v 26-28: Jesus' priesthood is different because he is perfect. His sinless life allowed him to do something no other priest could do: he offered up himself, becoming a sacrifice for our sins.

12. APPLY: What are the implications of this passage for someone who is...

- **frustrated by their own sin?** Jesus "always lives to make intercession" for us (v 25). This means that he will never stop forgiving us and pleading for us before God. We can have perfect confidence that he will deal with our sin.

- **doubtful or anxious?** This passage gives us many reasons to "hold fast to the hope set before us" (6:18). God promised Abraham descendants and he promised a new high priest in the order of Melchizedek. Both those promises have been kept. We can completely trust God.

- **feeling far away from God?** Although we may feel like we are far away from

God sometimes, the truth is that in Christ we never are. He "has gone as a forerunner on our behalf" into the heavenly throne room of God (v 20), which means that we too can be in God's presence. Because of Jesus, nothing can take that away.

6

Hebrews 8:1 – 10:25

A BETTER COVENANT

THE BIG IDEA

Sin is serious and our relationship with God is broken. But by his sacrifice on the cross, Jesus has solved this problem. We are fully forgiven and can draw near to God with confidence!

SUMMARY

Every human being is born a sinful person, estranged from God. The relationship is broken. In the Old Testament, God made a covenant with his people that enabled them to draw near to him through a system of sacrifices—but this was not perfect. There were many restrictions.

Hebrews 8 points out that this covenant was never God's final plan. It always pointed forward to Jesus. Verses 1-6 tell us that the old covenant temple was simply a symbol of the real dwelling place of God in heaven—which Jesus entered on our behalf. Verses 7-13 quote from Jeremiah 31 to show that God promised a new and better covenant. The implication is that this has been inaugurated by Christ.

Hebrews 9 develops these ideas. Verses 1-10 highlight the limitations of old covenant worship, which could not really deal with sin or allow people into God's presence. Verses 11-28 show how Jesus overcame those limitations—entering the true throne room of God and making a better sacrifice

which could bring true forgiveness and cleansing. This comparison between the old covenant and the new covenant shows us the seriousness of sin and the depth of God's love. It shows why Christ's sacrifice was necessary and what it achieved.

In 10:1-18, the author reminds us again that the old covenant was never entirely effective. It was always intended to be provisional and partial. But God had something better planned. Jesus' sacrifice has fulfilled the promises in Jeremiah 31: he has set us apart for God's service and forgiven our sins forever. Hebrews 10:19-25 concludes with a series of applications. The author urges us to draw near to God. This is the possibility which Jesus has achieved for us by his blood.

OPTIONAL EXTRA

Look at a diagram of the Old Testament tabernacle online. You can even build one out of card: have a look at www.visualunit.me/2015/01/21/the-tabernacle-mini-model

GUIDANCE FOR QUESTIONS

1. List some different types of agreement or contract people make with one another. What happens when they are broken? These could be trivial, like agreeing to meet up for a coffee, or very significant, like a marriage agreement or a legal contract—which may include penalties for breaking them. Explain to the group that in today's passage we will read that God entered into a covenant with his people. A biblical covenant is simply a binding agreement, in which two parties make vows to one another and exchange symbols associated with those promises.

2. Old covenant priests made offerings in the temple, which was originally a tent. What's the difference when it comes to Jesus' ministry (v 1-6)?

• The location is better. The tent set up by Moses is only "a copy and shadow of the heavenly things" (v 5). It was symbolic of the real dwelling place of God—which is where Jesus entered to do his work of mediation (v 1).
• The sacrifice is better (v 3). All priests must have "something to offer." But only Jesus offered himself.
• It was "enacted on better promises" (v 6). This is what the author explains in the following verses.

3. What had happened to the old covenant? God had loved the people of Israel and pledged himself to them—he "took them by the hand" (v 9) and rescued them from Egypt. But they were idolaters. Like a cheating spouse, they ran off with other gods. They broke their covenant.

• **What would this new covenant involve?**
  • New power. God would write his law on the people's hearts (v 10). That is, he would pour out his Holy Spirit and change them from the inside. New covenant people are empowered to obey God.
  • New people. There were many people in the nation of Israel under the old covenant who performed the rituals and kept the law but did not really believe.

So, the people of Israel often had to be told, "Know the Lord" (v 11). But under the new covenant, there is a revival, so that the knowledge of God spreads "from the least of them to the greatest."
• A new priest. God promises mercy and forgiveness (v 12). As the writer to the Hebrews has repeatedly told us, this is because of Jesus, our high priest.
NOTE: To be clear, sins were forgiven in Old Testament times too. But they were forgiven in anticipation of Christ's forthcoming work. It is in the new covenant that that forgiveness is finally secured.

• **Imagine you were an Israelite in Jeremiah's time. What would you have thought about this promise? Which part of it would you have been most excited about?** This question is designed to help you explore the passage in a different way. In Jeremiah's time, things in Israel were an utter shambles. The nation was divided into two kingdoms, exile was on the horizon, and idolatry was rampant. Given that setting, how do you think people felt to hear these promises?

4. What was the blood of animals used for under the old covenant (v 13)? Why is Jesus' blood more effective?

• The blood of animals achieved "the purification of the flesh" (v 13). We might call this ritual purity. It was symbolic, external purity.
• This meant that the high priest had to keep repeating this act of sacrifice (v 25). The blood of an animal could not change people on the inside, so they kept sinning.

- Jesus, by contrast, cleanses us internally. He sanctifies our hearts, not just our flesh (v 14).
- Jesus' blood was the perfect sacrifice. He is "without blemish" (v 14). So, he offered himself only once (v 26, 28).

5. What did Jesus' blood achieve (v 12, 14, 15, 26)?
- v 12, 26: He has secured "an eternal redemption" and "put away sin." We have been redeemed: our sins have been forgiven.
- v 14: He has enabled us "to serve the living God." We can now march into the presence of God, because our sins have been paid for.
- v 15: We have an "eternal inheritance." This includes our future resurrection. But the greatest part of the inheritance is Jesus himself. He is our great reward. We are looking forward to being with him eternally.

EXPLORE MORE
Read Genesis 2:16-17 and Romans 6:23. What is the result of sin here?
Fundamentally, sin leads to separation from God. In our sinful nature, we cannot draw near to God in this life—and we will be eternally separated from him when we die. That is the bigger picture behind these verses: the result of sin is death. It is not just physical death that is meant—it is the whole state of separation from God.
Read Leviticus 17:11. Why was animal blood used to atone for sin?
Blood symbolizes life. This is why animal blood was used in purification rituals. The animal's blood was given in place of a sinful human's life.
Read Matthew 26:28. Here Jesus' words echo Moses' words in Hebrews 9:20. What is the difference?

Jesus says, "This is my blood of the new covenant." He inaugurates the covenant in the same way that Moses did—but it is by a sacrifice of himself. This is the only blood that can really take away sin.

6. APPLY: We can now "serve the living God" and be "eagerly waiting" for Jesus' return (v 14, 28). What do those things mean for us today?
- Waiting for the Lord means looking forward to his return. We need to be longing for the day when our Lord returns to bring us home to himself at last.
- It also means serving God. After all, if we love Jesus then we will want to be like him. We have been cleansed; now we must turn away from our old lives of sin and seek to live as God would have us live, by the power of his Spirit.
- Many places in the New Testament urge us to be ready for the Lord's return. This is another way in which waiting for Jesus' return and serving God are linked. To explore this, you could look up Philippians 3:14-21; 2 Peter 3:10-14; Jude 20-23. These passages show that waiting eagerly for the Lord means living godly lives; encouraging one another in faith; telling unbelievers about Jesus; and setting our minds on heavenly things. Discuss with the group how you could put those things into practice this week.

- **What might prevent us from waiting eagerly?** Maybe we have simply become too comfortable—we stop looking forward to what is coming because we are enjoying what we have now. For some of us the reason is that we have become caught up in sin patterns which actually make us hope that Christ won't return anytime soon.

7. What did the old sacrificial system achieve, and what did it not achieve (v 1-4)? The sacrifices were "a reminder of sins every year" (v 3). The message couldn't be missed: you always need cleansing. But the blood of animals couldn't provide that cleansing (v 4). So, the sacrificial system also shows you that no effort you make, no matter how well-intended, could ever be enough to save you from your sins.

8. What was God's perspective on the sacrifices (v 5-7)? This quotation from Psalm 40 shows that the Old Testament itself acknowledged the limitations in the sacrificial system. Sacrifices were not enough.

- **These words are a quotation of Psalm 40:6-8. Christ was speaking through the psalmist (Hebrews 10:5). How do these words point to what Jesus would do?**
  - "A body have you prepared for me" (v 5) anticipates the incarnation. Christ would offer his own body.
  - "I have come to do your will" (v 7) reminds us that Jesus willingly, consciously, and intentionally gave himself for us.

9. In verses 15-17 the author highlights two of the promises God made in the prophecy of Jeremiah. How do verses 10-14 show that Jesus has fulfilled these promises?
- God's first promise is: "I will put my laws on their hearts, and write them on their minds" (v 16). This is what the author means by saying we have been sanctified (v 10). We have been cleansed by Christ once for all and set apart for his service. The Spirit works in us to make us more holy over time—empowering us to live more and more for Christ. (This

is why verse 14 says we are also "being sanctified.")
- God's second promise is: "I will remember their sins and their lawless deeds no more" (v 17). Jesus has made a single sacrifice for sins (v 10, 12, 14). This means there is no longer any need for animal sacrifices (v 18). Jesus' sacrifice is fully effectual and has brought total forgiveness.

10. Because of Jesus' sacrifice, what are we now able to do (v 19-22)?
- We can enter God's presence, the true "holy place" (v 19). This is because Jesus has made a way "through the curtain" (v 20). This is a reference to the curtain which blocked off the inner section of the temple.
- Instead of entering in fear, we can have "confidence" (v 19) and "full assurance" (v 22). This is because we have "a true heart" (v 22): we have been purified by Christ.

11. What will help us to take hold of this hope (v 23-25)?
- We can remember that "he who promised is faithful" (v 23). God is trustworthy in what he has promised. His word will prove true in the end.
- We need one another (v 24-25). Faith is one of those things you can't do alone. You need to be part of a team—with teammates who will help, encourage, push, rebuke, and love you, and whom you can help, encourage, push, rebuke, and love.

12. APPLY: Look back through Hebrews 8:1 – 10:25 and pick out a verse or verses which you might use to encourage someone who…
- **struggles with feelings of guilt.**
- **seeks assurance of their salvation.**

- **longs to be sure that God loves them.**
- **is confused about how the Old Testament relates to the New Testament.**
- **is repeatedly falling into sin.**
- **doubts what they believe about Jesus.**

You could divide the group up and give each person or pair of people one of these questions. Then ask them each to explain why the verse or verses they have chosen might help.

---

7 Hebrews 10:26 – 12:2
THE LIFE OF FAITH

THE BIG IDEA
Faith in Christ is the only way to please God. Faith is practical: it means looking to the future God has promised and persevering in obedience to God's ways.

SUMMARY
In Hebrews 10:22, our author urged us to draw near to God "in full assurance of faith." The remainder of chapter 10 builds on that: warning us not to turn our backs on our faith (v 26-31), the author tells us to look back at how far we've come (v 32-34) and forward to our ultimate goal (v 35-39). In the last verses of chapter 10, he calls us to live by faith. But what does that actually look like?

Hebrews 11 is sometimes known as the "Hall of Faith." It takes us through many Old Testament saints and reminds us what God can accomplish through his people when they trust him. But it is really about the object of our faith. Hebrews 11 calls us to trust in God and look to the future he has promised.

After starting with a definition of faith (v 1), our author fleshes out that definition with three examples—Abel, Enoch, and Noah (v 2-7). Each of them highlights a different aspect of faith, but all have one thing in common: their faith pleased God.

Verses 8-12 focus on Abraham, another example of faith. God promised Abraham that the land of Canaan would become the inheritance of his many descendants—so Abraham obediently went there. But although he received the promise of many descendants, he never got to see the day when they would inhabit the promised land. Verses 13-16 tell us that Abraham obeyed because he had faith in something greater than the promised land. He—along with other Old Testament saints—was "looking forward" to a different land altogether: a heavenly city, not an earthly one.

Verses 17-38 continue a review of Old Testament figures of faith, from Abraham onward. Again and again we see these figures persevering in obedience to God because they were looking forward to what he had promised—even when that perseverance meant suffering. Yet verse 39 reminds us that "all these, though commended through their faith, did not receive what was promised." Does that mean their faith was meaningless? No. God has provided "something better." In Christ, all the earlier promises finally come to fruition. In Christ, these Old Testament saints can at last be "made perfect" along with all who believe.

"Therefore … let us run with endurance the race that is set before us," continues Hebrews 12:1. Our author calls us to persevere in living for God, just like all the examples he cited in chapter 11. His final example is Jesus himself—but Jesus is not just another member of the "Hall of Faith." He is "the founder and perfecter of our faith" (12:2). It is only because of him that we can run the race of faith at all. When we are "looking forward" to our heavenly reward, we are looking to Christ.

OPTIONAL EXTRA

Read out the following scenarios. For each one, ask your group to vote on which character has more genuine or more admirable faith—then ask them why they chose that answer! Be warned: they may not be straightforward… The point is to explore and discuss what faith really means.

- Jane flies her small single-engine airplane to America's east coast and looks out over the Atlantic. She doesn't have much fuel in her tank, but she decides to try to head for England. Jim is also going to England—on a jumbo jet. He is terrified of flying and is convinced that the plane will crash. But he gets on board anyway.
- Al will only believe what he sees evidence for. He reads lots of books and comes to the conclusion that Jesus really is the Son of God. Anna has grown up in a Christian home and has never really thought intellectually about Jesus—she just knows she loves him and will do anything for him.
- Marvin has exams coming up. He hasn't bothered to do much revision, but he has faith in himself—he's sure he'll do well. Melanie is really worried about the exams.

She has worked hard and her teachers seem to think she'll pass, but she does some extra revision anyway, just in case.
- Gabriella and Ben are ten-year-old twins. Their parents have promised to buy them an ice cream if they behave well all day. Ben does his best to behave, but Gabriella doesn't bother—surely if she pulls her sweetest smile at the end of the day, she'll get an ice cream anyway?

GUIDANCE FOR QUESTIONS

1. If you asked 100 people what the word "faith" means, what answers do you think you would get? What is helpful or unhelpful about those answers? Our world loves to talk about faith (think Oprah Winfrey) and even sing about it (think George Michael). As far as Western culture is concerned, faith is a feeling, a positive outlook on life. Often people talk about having faith in yourself— becoming who you're really meant to be. But this idea does not really stand up to scrutiny. Faith just becomes something that you conjure up in yourself. It is something to add to the list of things that we need to do. And if true faith is all about looking inward and seeing how great I am, that is not such good news. I'm a mess! The biblical definition of faith is radically different. It is not just about being a positive thinker. We are called to take our trust and place it in something outside ourselves.

EXPLORE MORE
Read Hebrews 10:26-31. These verses say that anyone who knows about the grace of God in Christ, yet stubbornly embraces sin, is actively rejecting Christ. Why is this so serious?
- We have learned in previous chapters that Jesus is the only way we can safely stand before a holy God. If you reject

him, there is no other way. So "there no longer remains a sacrifice for sins" (v 26). Instead there will be judgment (v 27) and vengeance (v 30).

- The punishment for those who have been part of the community of faith, then spurned Christ, will be even worse than the punishment for other sinners (v 28-29).

NOTE: A true Christian cannot lose their salvation. But God uses warnings like this to make us examine our faith and help us press on. It is possible to be part of the church and believe intellectually in Christ, without being a true disciple. For more on this, see *Hebrews For You*, pages 150-151; also pages 53-54, 77-78, and 85-91.

Read Hebrews 10:32-39. Our author is addressing the original readers directly here. How have they shown faith in the past (v 32-34)?

- They were willing to endure suffering (v 32).
- They loved others (v 33-34).
- They had joy in their hearts (v 34) because they were looking forward to their reward in Christ.

What will be the result of their faith if they persevere (v 35-39)?

- They will gain a "great reward" (v 35).
- This is not a reward that is earned. Nor is it money or other material wealth. It is the gift of eternal life in heaven (v 39).

2. What does faith involve (v 1)?

- Faith is not just a feeling. It means being certain about something. It is rock-solid trust that when God makes a promise, it is true and right.
- "Things hoped for" are things in the future that have not yet happened. "Things not seen" are things in the past which we weren't there to see. Or, put simply, our faith is in what God has done and what God will do.

- **Why is faith so important (v 2, 6)?**
  We please God by faith. This has always been true for God's people. It is only by faith that anyone, in any time, can be considered righteous in the eyes of God. Of course, we must be clear about what we mean when we say we "please" God by our faith. Faith is not a good work that God rewards. Faith is the instrument by which we receive the thing that saves, namely Christ. Since God is pleased with Christ, he is pleased with us.

3. What did faith look like in the lives of Abel (look up Genesis 4:1-12), Enoch (Genesis 5:18-24), and Noah (Genesis 6:9 – 7:24)?

- Abel brought a pleasing sacrifice to God. He enjoyed God's favor because he approached him in the right way.
- Enoch was close to God—he "walked with God" (Genesis 5:22, 24). His faith meant that he had a personal, daily relationship with God.
- Noah believed God's warnings. God gave him a command which made no sense on a human level—to build a huge boat in the middle of the dry land. Noah obeyed "in reverent fear." He was made "an heir of righteousness" and was accepted by God (Hebrews 11:7).

4. What was the reward for each of these figures?

- Most importantly, God was pleased with them. He commended each one of them and made them righteous—that is, they became righteous in his sight. That cannot be because they were truly righteous in their own strength. Nor is faith a righteous action in itself. Rather, it is through faith in Christ that we can become righteous in God's sight. This applies to Old Testament figures as much as it does to us today, because the whole Old Testament looks forward to Christ.

- Abel "still speaks"—in the sense that the lesson of his life is still applicable today.
- Enoch did not die an earthly death.
- Noah saved his family.

5. APPLY: What would it look like today for us to have faith like Abel, Enoch, and Noah?

- Abel approached God in the way God wanted. We must approach God through Christ alone.
- Enoch had a personal relationship with God. The Christian life is not just about believing certain truths. Faith means drawing near to God and seeking him. We should invest time with God as we would with any other person—spending time in prayer and Bible reading on a regular basis.
- Noah obeyed God even when it didn't seem to make sense. We must trust that God is right and obey him even when we don't understand.

6. What did Abraham do because of his faith (v 8-9)? Abraham obeyed God's call to leave his home and journey to a foreign land (see Genesis 12). This required faith because he didn't know "where he was going" (v 8)! Even so, he obeyed.

⌄

- **How did Abraham's wife Sarah show faith (v 11-12)?** Sarah believed God's promise that she would have a child—even though she was "past the age" of conceiving a child (v 11) and her husband was "as good as dead" (v 12)! The result was that she and Abraham had many descendants (v 12).

7. What was Abraham looking forward to (v 8, 10, 13-16)?

- v 8: Abraham believed God's promise that the land of Canaan would one day become the inheritance of Abraham's many descendants.
- v 10: But he was really looking forward to a different land altogether. His hope was in a future eternal city—a heavenly home, not an earthly one.
- v 13: This is why Abraham acknowledged that he was a foreigner. He was still "seeking a homeland" (v 14), even when he was living in the land God had promised.
- v 16: He was seeking "a better country, that is, a heavenly one." Abraham (and the other figures our author has mentioned) wanted most of all to be with God. So God has prepared a place for them to be with him.

8. In verses 17-19 there is another example from the life of Abraham. By faith, he obeyed God's command to offer up his only son, Isaac, as a sacrifice. Why was it difficult for Abraham to have faith and obey? At the most obvious level, this boy was Abraham's only son. No doubt he loved him more than life itself. To give up your own child—for what seemed like no good reason—might be the hardest test anyone could ever face. Beyond this, God's command seemed out of sync with his earlier promises. Isaac was the one through whom the rest of Abraham's offspring was supposed to come (v 18). If Isaac died, how could God keep his promise?

- **What enabled Abraham to obey (v 19)?** Abraham obeyed because he believed that God could bring Isaac back to life if necessary. He was sure that God would keep his promise.

9. Look at some of the other figures the author mentions. How did each one show faith? What were they looking forward to? You could split the group into three for this question and ask each to focus on one figure.

- **Joseph (v 22; see Genesis 50:24-25)** Joseph's faith was displayed at the end of his life. He believed that the people would one day be delivered from Egypt, and he wanted them to take his bones with them to the promised land.

- **Moses (v 23-28)**
  - Moses was raised by Pharaoh's daughter, yet he refused the pleasures and wealth of Egypt (v 24-25). He resisted temptation because he believed that the pleasures that were presented to him were fleeting. Instead he looked to what would last. He knew real pleasure and true wealth come from trusting in Jesus.
  - Moses was not afraid of Pharaoh because he believed there was someone greater, the "invisible" God of the universe (v 27).
  - He obeyed God by keeping the Passover (v 28). This was the way God delivered Moses and the Israelites out of the hands of an angry Pharaoh: he sent "the Destroyer of the firstborn" into Egypt and told the Israelites to sprinkle blood on their doorposts so that they would be protected.

- **Rahab (v 31; see Joshua 2)** Rahab was an inhabitant of Jericho who helped Israelite spies to escape from the city. She did this because she knew where God's favor lay (Joshua 2:9). Her faith was in God's power to destroy the city. Because she helped them, she was saved.

10. How would you summarize the experience of people of faith in verses 32-34? What about in verses 35-38?

- v 32-34: Faith allows God's people to accomplish amazing things. These figures trusted God and he chose to work powerfully in their lives. You could look up some of these figures if you have time. Gideon defeated the Midianites with only 300 men (Judges 7). Barak was a great general under Deborah (Judges 4). Samson famously defeated the Philistines (Judges 13 – 16). Jephthah was a great warrior (Judges 11). David was God's king. Samuel and the prophets spoke for God and upheld truth. "Stopped the mouths of lions" refers to Samson in Judges 14:6-7 and David in 1 Samuel 17:34-36; "quenched the power of fire" is likely a reference to Shadrach, Meshach, and Abednego in Daniel 3.

- v 35-38: Faith also means being willing to endure suffering. Or, to put it another way, the only people willing to suffer in this way are people of faith, who value and love Jesus more than anything. We can connect most of the things in this list to individual stories in the Old Testament, or to traditions outside the Old Testament. Many of the prophets endured torture, mocking, and imprisonment—especially Jeremiah (Jeremiah 20:1-2; 38). The prophet Zechariah was stoned (2 Chronicles 24:20-21) and other historical sources tell us that Isaiah may have been sawn in two. Various figures were on the run in deserts or caves (1 Samuel 22:1; 1 Kings 19:4).

- **Why do you think our author showed both types of experience?** This is a warning for us to temper our expectations of what the life of faith is like. God does not promise that if we follow him we will have health and wealth—becoming successful or rich. It is better to follow Jesus; but that does not mean bigger bank accounts or more popularity. This is not your best life now.

11. Look at verse 2. How is Jesus' example of faith similar to the figures mentioned in chapter 11?

- Jesus showed great endurance, just like the Old Testament figures who suffered a great deal. He persevered in faith.
- This was because he was looking forward to his heavenly reward ("the joy that was set before him"), just like Abraham and others in chapter 11.

- **But why is Jesus better than any other example of faith?**
    - Jesus is not just an example for us to follow. He is "the founder and perfecter of our faith." He is the one who makes it possible for us to have faith, and he is the one who brings our faith to completion—who runs the race for us so that we might follow in his footsteps.
    - Jesus has received his reward: he is "seated at the right hand of the throne of God." He makes it possible for us—and for all those Old Testament figures—to be beside the throne of heaven one day too.

12. APPLY: 10:36 says, "You have need of endurance, so that when you have done the will of God you may receive what is promised." According to 12:1-2, how can we make sure we persevere in obedient faith?

- We can look to the Old Testament figures mentioned in chapter 11 (the "cloud of witnesses") to remind us that it really is possible to finish the race of faith.
- We must "lay aside every weight" (12:1). This means we need to make sure that anything that could trip us up or drag us back is stripped off. This includes things that are not sinful in themselves but

distract us from our faith.
- We must also strip off the "sin which clings so closely." We all make mistakes, but we must own them, repent of them, and turn from them onto new pathways of obedience.
- We must look to Jesus. Remember that we are in the race only because Jesus has entered us, and he will sustain us. Keep praying for his help.

13. Here are some things which make it hard to persevere in faith. For each one, how might the verses in brackets help a person in that situation?

- **Struggling to believe God is there at all (11:1-3).**
- **Falling into the trap of seeking to please God by other means than faith in Christ (11:4-6).**
- **Feeling insecure and uncertain about life (11:8-10).**
- **Struggling to believe that God really means what he says (11:11-12, 17-19).**
- **Not wanting to obey God's commands (11:17-19).**
- **Being distracted by other things (11:16, 24-26).**
- **Being afraid (11:27-29).**
- **Feeling unworthy or insignificant (11:32-34).**
- **Suffering (10:34; 11:35-40).**
- **Becoming weighed down by sin (12:1).**
It may be helpful to divide the group up into pairs. Ask each pair to look up one or two of the verses from the list and then report back to the group.

8 Hebrews 12:3 – 13:25
A KINGDOM THAT CANNOT BE SHAKEN

THE BIG IDEA

Pursue holiness and endure suffering because in Christ you have something that cannot be shaken: a heavenly kingdom and an eternal home.

SUMMARY

The Christian life involves perseverance. Our author's original audience have been facing all sorts of challenges, but he urges them not to grow weary (12:3-4). Why? First of all, he interprets the situation for them. God has allowed this suffering as a way of training these believers (v 5-11). When they suffer, they should remember that God is a Father seeking their good. He is also like a coach, training them hard to make them more righteous. So, they shouldn't respond to suffering by quitting but by persevering (v 12-17).

But the issue is not just whether we are running, but whether we are running toward the right finish line. In Hebrews 12:18-24, our author uses a new image to describe what Christians are running toward: Mount Zion, which represents the heavenly city of God. He first discusses Mount Sinai, which represents the old covenant: this was the mountain which Moses climbed in Exodus 19 – 20 to receive the Ten Commandments. This mountain was terrifying: the people could not go near it because God was so holy. Then our author switches to Mount Zion. Christians are now made perfect because of Christ's sacrifice. We can come safely and joyfully

into God's presence. This is the finish line in the Christian life.

But God is still the same God—"a consuming fire" (v 29)—and he holds us responsible for following the new covenant. We are warned (v 25-29) that Christ will return to "shake" the world. We have access to a kingdom that cannot be shaken, but only by God's grace through Jesus—so we must worship him with reverence.

Hebrews 13 gets down to brass tacks. What does it actually look like day-to-day to persevere in living a holy life?

- v 1-6: A Christian should be outward-focused, looking to care for those around them, and also look inward at their own life, faith, and morality.
- v 7, 17: Our leaders are there to help us pursue a life of faith.
- v 8-10: These verses warn us away from false teaching: we are cleansed by Jesus' blood alone.
- v 11-14: Jesus suffered for us just like an Old Testament animal sacrifice. So we must be willing to endure reproach for his sake.
- v 15-16: We are called to praise and to good works—the natural outflowing of the gospel of grace. The author refers to these as a form of "sacrifice," highlighting again the difference between the covenants. We don't sacrifice animals, but we sacrifice our lives.

The letter closes with a personal request for prayer (v 18-19), a benediction or blessing (v 20-21), and some final greetings (v 22-25).

The last statement is a short blessing: "Grace be with all of you." This is a fitting end to the book of Hebrews, whose message has been that salvation is earned by the shed blood of Jesus Christ. Only his blood enables us to "draw near to the throne of grace" (4:16).

OPTIONAL EXTRA

Choose two simple physical activities that you can do in the space you have (for example, bouncing a tennis ball on a racquet or throwing and catching in pairs). Each activity should be as different as possible from the other. Divide everyone into two teams and see how many times they can do each activity in 30 seconds. Then make each group practice only one of the activities for five minutes. At the end of the five minutes, run the competitions again. Hopefully, each group will have improved on the activity that they practiced! Make the point that training is a vital part of any sport. It develops our skills and builds our endurance. In the first part of today's passage, Christians are compared to athletes. God disciplines us— he trains us—to build our faith and help us keep going.

GUIDANCE FOR QUESTIONS

1. What things make people grow weary or fainthearted in their Christian life? It could be hostility from unbelievers (this, as we'll see, is what the author's original audience were enduring). It could be complacency or boredom, when we feel "stuck" in our faith and find it hard to see the glorious truths of the gospel with fresh eyes. It could be suffering and trouble in life. It could also be due to temptation or struggling with sin. Ultimately, we grow weary when we forget to fix our eyes on the finish line—our final reward of being with Jesus forever in the new creation.

2. God is like a father (v 5-11). What is the purpose of his discipline? God's discipline reminds us that we are God's children (v 6). He is doing it because he loves us. It is for our good, because it changes us—refining us to make us more holy (v 10) and righteous (v 11).

- **Why is suffering therefore a good sign (v 7-8)?** A life of trials is not a sign that God is out to get you, but that he is out to love you. "God is treating you as sons" (v 7). The opposite is also true. Physical comfort and ease might actually be a sign that God is displeased with you. Sometimes God lets the wicked prosper and have a life of ease (Psalm 73). He gives sinners over to their sin and allows them to do what they want (Romans 1:22-32)—at least for a time.

3. God's discipline is like athletic training (v 11-13). How should we respond— and what does that response actually look like (v 14-17)? A common reaction to suffering is to give up. But our author encourages us not to (v 12)! He also tells us to "make straight paths for your feet" (v 13). In other words, stay in the lane you are running in. Do not divert from the track of righteousness and obedience. This means:

- v 14: Pursuing peace with one another, as well as holiness (a godly life).
- v 15: Keeping others on the path too. We pray for one another and support one another to make sure that we are all running to Jesus. We make sure that no "root of bitterness" springs up to cause trouble. This is an allusion to Deuteronomy 29:18, where the root of bitterness is a person who abandons the way of the Lord and leads others astray. The point, then, is to be on watch for one another so that apostates don't arise and harm the body of Christ.

- v 16: Refusing to pursue sinful pleasures. Esau sacrificed his long-term standing (his "birthright" of blessing from God) for short-term pleasure (a "single meal"). Verse 17 does not mean that God denies a person a chance to repent even when they wish to do so. The lesson is that pursuing short-term pleasure can have long-term consequences that cannot be undone. Sometimes the opportunity to turn away from your rebellion passes you by (see Hebrews 6:4-6).

4. Compare Mount Sinai with Mount Zion.

- **What kind of place is each mountain (v 18, 22, 25)?** Mount Sinai is a physical, earthly place, characterized by fear. But Mount Zion is a heavenly place, characterized by joyful celebration.

- **Who is able to go to each mountain (v 20-21, 22-23)?** At Mount Sinai, God ordered that no one come near. If even an animal touched the mountain, it would be struck dead. Moses was able to go up the mountain, but even he was terrified. Mount Zion is completely different. It is not only angels who are welcome there. Addressing his readers, the author says, "You have come to Mount Zion." Christians are there—"the firstborn" and "the righteous made perfect." Because of Jesus, sinful people who could not go near to God at Mount Sinai are now able to draw near.

- **God has not changed between Mount Sinai and Mount Zion. He is still " a consuming fire" (v 29). So what has changed?** We have Jesus, the mediator of a new covenant (the new way of relating to God which we saw in Study 6). The thunder of the law has been hushed, because Jesus has satisfied it. It is Christ's blood that cleanses us and allows us to be received without fear by God.

EXPLORE MORE
Read Genesis 4:8-11. What do you think the blood of Abel cries out to God? Abel's blood cries out to God for justice. The result was that Cain was cursed. Abel's blood thus reminds us that God upholds his holy standards by bringing judgment. **Christ's blood also "speaks" to God. What "better word" do you think it says?** Christ's blood cries out for mercy. It says, "I have died for them. Show them grace."

5. At Mount Sinai, God's voice made the earth shake. Now he has promised to shake things again (v 26). What does this mean (v 27)? This is a citation of Haggai 2:6. The shaking is a picture of God's promise to judge the nations. That promise is fulfilled in Christ, who will be the judge of all the world when he returns. He will sift eternal things from temporal, created things ("things that have been made"). All earthly kingdoms, all worldly powers and authorities, will be defeated and overthrown.

- **What will remain (v 28)?** God's kingdom will remain. This includes all that has been done for Christ in this world (see 1 Corinthians 3:11-15).

6. APPLY: How should we respond to the knowledge that Jesus will one day shake the heavens and the earth (v 25, 28)? This is a warning: "See that you do not refuse him who is speaking" (v 25). If we fall away from Christ, we too will be shaken. Remembering that should motivate us to give our all for Christ. But it is also good news! We are receiving "a kingdom that cannot be shaken" (v 28). We must worship

God with gratitude.

- **How does this help us to persevere in faith and pursue holiness even when times are hard or when we are tempted by other things?** We only have one way of gaining access to God's heavenly kingdom: Jesus. Knowing this should motivate us to press on in faith—partly because the consequences for falling away are so dreadful, and partly because the reward for persevering is so wonderful. No suffering we can endure on earth will be as great as God's final judgment on sinners who have not given their lives to Christ. This is a reason to press on even when times are hard. No pleasure we can enjoy on earth will be as great as the pleasure of being in God's heavenly city eternally. This is a reason to press on even when we are tempted by other things. Practically speaking, spending time in praise and worship is vital for building our faith and keeping our eyes on the goal.

7. APPLY: How do you—as a church, and as individuals—usually approach God in prayer and worship? How can you make sure you do so with gratitude, reverence, and awe (v 28)?

- Consider together how you could grow in gratitude. The most important thing is to reflect often on God's grace. When we grasp the extraordinary grace that allows us to come to Mount Zion and Christ, we will be full of gratitude. It's also worth making an effort to be aware of all that God gives us every day. You could write down prayers to help you keep track of when God has answered them. Or write out lists of things you are thankful for.
- Think, too, about how you can make sure gratitude is a key feature of your prayers together. What proportion of your prayer or worship times are spent simply praising

God? It may be helpful to deliberately set aside the first portion of your prayer time just for thank-you prayers.

- Our worship should also have gravity. Often, we are very familiar with God, because we know he is our friend and Father. But it is also healthy to remember that God is "a consuming fire" of holiness (v 29). Expressions of awe and respect could include kneeling or standing to pray; confessing sins before moving onto requests; and reading or reciting more formal prayers (for example, the prayers of historical figures).

8. In verses 1-6, our author urges us to pursue love and godliness. Who should we love and how (v 1-3)?

- v 1: The umbrella thought here is the concept of "brotherly love." In Christ, all believers are brothers and sisters. We should love one another accordingly.
- v 2: We should show hospitality. Early Christians traveled a great deal. This was to "network" among Christians, as well as to spread the gospel. So, the "strangers" our author has in view are likely Christian missionaries.
- v 3: We should care for those who are persecuted for their faith. In the early church it was very common for Christians to be jailed just for being Christians. Caring for people in prison was therefore the need of the hour. The principle that is mainly in view is that we should help those who are suffering persecution as a result of their faith. We should have compassion on those who are suffering physically because we also have physical bodies!

- **How else should we pursue godliness, and why (v 4-6)?**
  - v 4: Marriage must be honored and sexual immorality avoided. God will judge sexual immorality. This does not

mean that there is no forgiveness for those of us who have sexual sin in our past or are struggling with sexual sin in the present. There is always forgiveness for those who repent of their sin, believe in Christ, and commit to living for him. It is the person who defies God directly and refuses to repent that God will judge for his or her sexual immorality.

- We do not apply this verse by walking out into the world and condemning everybody who is sexually immoral. We start by applying it to our own lives.

- v 5: We should be content and not seek wealth. Having money is not sinful in itself. But pursuing money (whether you are rich or poor) prevents us from trusting God for what we need. God has said, "I will never leave you nor forsake you." If you really believe that, you will not be so worried about money.

9. Verses 7 and 17 talk about Christian leaders. How does God use leaders in our lives?

- Leaders teach us (v 7). Hearing God's word from our leaders is the central way that God wants us to learn from him. This is one reason why it is so important to be part of a regular church congregation.

- They are there as examples of faith (v 7).

- They are shepherds of our souls, keeping watch over us. God has given them responsibility over us and they will one day "have to give an account" for our faith.

- **What should our attitude be toward them?**

  - We should watch and imitate them (v 7)—insofar as they imitate Christ (1 Corinthians 11:1).

  - We should obey and submit to them (v 17). They are our guides and shepherds. They are the ones whom God has placed over us. Of course, we are not called to follow our leaders blindly. If they are taking you down a sinful or heretical path, you are called to avoid them. If they are authoritarian or abusive, they must be exposed for the false shepherds they are. But most church leaders are faithful shepherds who are doing the best they can. They have a heavy burden to look after us and lead us well. We should submit to them so that they can lead us "with joy and not with groaning."

EXPLORE MORE

What comparison does he make in verses 11-12? The author compares Jesus' sacrifice with Old Testament sacrifices. When a sin offering was made, the priests would take the bodies of the victims and burn them outside the camp. This was an important symbolic gesture. To be in the camp was to be near God; to be outside the camp was to be rejected by God. Putting animal sacrifices outside the camp was a sign that the judgment the people deserved had been diverted. The animals had been rejected outside the camp, but the people could stay inside the camp and draw near to God. So, it is significant that "Jesus also suffered outside the gate" (v 12). He took on God's displeasure and was cast out of the city, taking the place of those who should have been rejected.

What does he urge us to do in response (v 13)? We are to "go to him outside the camp and bear the reproach he endured." Jesus took all this reproach and rejection for us. Are we willing to be associated with him? Are we willing to be associated with that sort of shame and humiliation? Because of Jesus, we will never suffer rejection by God. This should make us willing to endure scorn from others.

10. We please God by faith in Jesus (11:6)—not by making animal sacrifices. But in verses 15-16 our author talks about two other kinds of sacrifice. What are they, and why are they expressions of faith?

• We should "offer up a sacrifice of praise" (v 15). Praise is "the fruit of lips that acknowledge his name." In other words, it is the result of faith. If we believe in Jesus, we will praise him.

• We should also "do good and to share what [we] have." Again, good works are the natural outflowing of faith. Because we are looking forward to "the city that is to come" (v 14), we are able to sacrifice our possessions, time, and money now, for the sake of others.

11. APPLY: Our author's application boils down to these three commands: endure suffering and reproach (v 13), praise God (v 15), and do good (v 16). Which do you think is hardest? What specific things can you do to apply each of these commands in your own life?

Encourage the group to think concretely about what each of these things looks like in your own context. What hardships are you or people you know enduring? How could you encourage one another to praise God more? What good needs to be done in your community?

12. APPLY: Think back over the whole of the time you have spent looking at the book of Hebrews. How would you sum up its message? If you had to choose one take-home point for your own life, what would it be? Different people may emphasize different things they have found helpful. But any summary of the book of Hebrews should include the line: "Jesus is better." He is more glorious and more worthy of worship than anything else. When compared with the way people were able to relate to God in the Old Testament, Jesus brings a better hope (7:19), a better covenant (7:22; 8:6), better promises (8:6), a better sacrifice (9:23), and a better country (11:16). He is better than we ever could have imagined.

The Good Book Guide Series

There are more than 50 Good Book Guides to explore, covering much of the Old Testament and New Testament besides many topical studies.

Find them at:

thegoodbook.com | thegoodbook.co.uk
thegoodbook.com.au | thegoodbook.co.nz | thegoodbook.co.in

the good book
COMPANY

BIBLICAL | RELEVANT | ACCESSIBLE

At The Good Book Company, we are dedicated to helping Christians and local churches grow. We believe that God's growth process always starts with hearing clearly what he has said to us through his timeless word—the Bible.

Ever since we opened our doors in 1991, we have been striving to produce Bible-based resources that bring glory to God. We have grown to become an international provider of user-friendly resources to the Christian community, with believers of all backgrounds and denominations using our books, Bible studies, devotionals, evangelistic resources, and DVD-based courses.

We want to equip ordinary Christians to live for Christ day by day, and churches to grow in their knowledge of God, their love for one another, and the effectiveness of their outreach.

Call us for a discussion of your needs or visit one of our local websites for more information on the resources and services we provide.

Your friends at The Good Book Company

thegoodbook.com | thegoodbook.co.uk
thegoodbook.com.au | thegoodbook.co.nz
thegoodbook.co.in